# SHIFT

# SHIFT

## Change Your *Words*,
## Change Your *World*

JANET SMITH WARFIELD

Las Vegas, Nevada

LCCN 2006905385

Publisher's Cataloging-in-Publication
(*Provided by Quality Books, Inc.*)

Warfield, Janet Smith.
Shift : *change your words, change your world*/Janet Smith Warfield.—1st ed.
p. cm.

Includes bibliographical references and index.
ISBN: 978-0-9778324-6-0 (cloth)
ISBN: 978-0-9778324-7-7 (paper)

1.  Spiritual life—Miscellanea.
2.  Self-actualization (Psychology)—Religious aspects—Miscellanea.
3.  Consciousness—Miscellanea.
I.  Title.

BL624.W346 2007          204´.4
                                    QBI06-600134

# Contents

# About the Author

Thirty-five years ago, Janet Smith Warfield had a mystical experience. Words she had been taught in Sunday School, "... resist not evil: but whosoever shall smite thee on thy right cheek, turn to him the other also" suddenly became crystal clear. What had seemed like an impossible moral commandment suddenly became a win/win solution.

Janet soon discovered the difficulty of expressing the mystical experience in words. The experience brought certainty, the words expressing it, uncertainty. Did she know or didn't she know?

For thirty-five years, Janet has been honing her language and people skills so that others may experience the exhilarating consciousness shift that she experienced. As mother, grandmother, poet, mediator, lawyer, and author, she has learned how to ask the right questions to uncover the right answers.

What did the masters do with words? They created.

What does Janet do with words? She creates. Creativity is the only reason we are here on this earth.

Janet is a graduate of Swarthmore College and Rutgers School of Law, Camden, with honors. She practiced law in Atlantic City, New Jersey, for twenty-two years.

# Preface—To the Reader

This is an exciting time to be alive. The world is exploding in exponential growth.

We stand on the brink of a precipice. Our knowledge will either destroy us or guide us to a peaceful, prosperous planet. The line between the two is razor thin.

Words and how we use them are major parts of our challenge. Words are creative vehicles. They are not Truth. We can, however, use them to sharpen our focus, expand our thinking, and transform our planet.

In this book, I use words in many ways. I tell stories. I write poems. I ask questions. I give commands. All are simply different ways of using words. None is Truth. All are only catalysts to your own thinking. I have differentiated the ways I use words through changes in formatting. Use what helps. Discard what does not.

Creating a peaceful earth is not a top-down job. It is a bottom-up job. Are you part of this creativity? Of course you are! To succeed, it requires the participation of every person on this planet.

So put on your creative hat, sharpen your mind, and let's begin.

Janet Smith Warfield
Roatan, Honduras

# Acknowledgments

Thousands of individuals have contributed to this book. Every person who has touched my life, even in the smallest way, has shaped the production of this manuscript. I can't thank you enough for the life you have given to the words in this book.

I give special thanks to Judy Yero, Lynn Stiles, Ann Elliott, Rachel Goddard, Helen Berliner, Amber Grady, Simon Filtness, Delmae Bower, Chris Igwe, Jae Rang, Amy Sosnov, and Gary Smith for brainstorming and editing content; Dick Margulis for cover design, book design, and typography; Random House, Inc., for permission to use the quotation by Kahlil Gibran; Jae Malone for permission to use her words about words; and John Langdon and the Estate of M.C. Escher for permission to use some amazing artwork.

Many of the poems in this book have been previously published. In some cases, the poems have been revised since their earlier publications. "Global Harmony" was previously published in *One Earth* from The Findhorn Foundation and Community. "Today" and "Doormat" were previously published in *Nanny Fanny Poetry Magazine,* Felicity Press, and *Feelings,* Anderie Poetry Press. "Today" was also published in Write On! (*Write On 2: Selected Works of Jersey Cape Writers*).

"Dawn," "Rain," and portions of "Perspective" were previously published in *The Best 100 Poems of Beauty, Faith and Inspiration*, Anderie Poetry Press. "Blessings" was previously published in *Poems of Beauty, Faith and Inspiration*, Anderie Poetry Press, and on the Online Noetic Network. "Monastery of the Soul" was previously published by The Atlantic City Free Public Library as part of its First Annual Poetry Reading. "Babylon" and "Haiku Couplets (If)" were previously published in *Feelings*, Anderie Poetry Press. "Perspective" was previously published under the title "Quadruplets" in *Feelings*, Anderie Poetry Press. "Haiku" (teacher and student) was previously published in *Feelings*, Anderie Poetry Press.

# Warning—Disclaimer

DO NOT READ THIS BOOK UNLESS YOU CAN COPE WITH CONTROVERSIAL IDEAS. NEITHER JANET SMITH WARFIELD NOR WORD SCULPTURES™ PUBLISHING, L.P. WILL TAKE ANY RESPONSIBILITY WHATSOEVER FOR YOUR EMOTIONAL REACTIONS TO THE BLACK MARKS ON THESE WHITE PIECES OF PAPER. YOUR REACTIONS ARE YOUR RESPONSIBILITY! IF YOU CAN'T DEAL WITH THE CONTENT OF THIS BOOK IN A RESPONSIBLE, NON-VIOLENT MANNER, DON'T READ IT! IF YOU CHOOSE TO READ IT...

Don't believe a word I write! My words are not Truth. They are only creative vehicles for discovering your own truth.

Read every statement with a dash of skepticism. There will be times when these statements won't apply to your life. You are the only one who can decide when they do and when they don't.

Play with my words the way you would play with a new toy or game. Allow your own creative spirit to tweak them and re-shape them. If you discover something that might be useful, use it. If you don't, let it go. It may make sense some other time in some other context.

While I hate to add the following statement, I am a former attorney, so here goes:

Read this book at your own risk. By reading these words, you agree that neither Janet Smith Warfield nor Word Sculptures™ Publishing shall have any liability whatsoever to any person or legal entity for any loss or damage caused, or alleged to have been caused, directly or indirectly, by any ideas or information contained in this book. If you do not wish to accept this, please return the book immediately to the publisher for a full refund.

# SHIFT

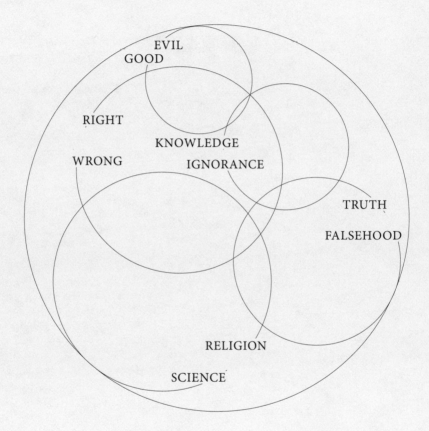

EVIL
GOOD

RIGHT

KNOWLEDGE

WRONG        IGNORANCE

TRUTH

FALSEHOOD

RELIGION

SCIENCE

# PART ONE

## *Words That Suddenly Shifted*

჻

## Metamorphosis

Strangled, suffocated,
by words, thoughts, teachings,

my mind lets go, and

I, cradled in now,
absorb the sunset's soothing pinks and reds
each moment unrepeated

breathing again

a tiny speck of eternity.

# 1

# The Mystical Experience

## *How It All Began*

The mysteries of life become lucid... and often,
nay usually, the solution is more or less unutterable
in words. —WILLIAM JAMES

I DON'T REMEMBER WHO came to my door. I don't remember
what he said. I do remember he was angry, arrogant, and rude.

I had just finished reading a book called *Summerhill* by an
English schoolmaster, A.S. Neill. Its theme was "freedom, not
license." Each student in Neill's school was free to do what he
wanted as long as he didn't hurt anyone. The community Neill
had created was a free, creative, loving, respectful, responsible
interaction of unique human beings.

The behavior of the man at the door was obnoxious, but he
wasn't hurting me. I decided to allow him to vent his anger. I
didn't do it because it was something I ought to do. I did it because I chose to do it. I experienced acceptance of the anger and
no desire to retaliate. Suddenly, the anger stopped.

Nothing changed. My house, the door, the living room, the
man, were all still there, just as they had been five minutes before.

Yet everything changed. Suddenly, I understood the meaning of words I'd been taught as a child: "But I say unto you, that ye resist not evil; but whosoever shall smite thee on thy right cheek, turn to him the other also." (Matt. 6:39)

My five-year-old son Bill began wetting the bed after his youngest brother was born. This new, irritating behavior made hours of extra work for me at a time when I was already exhausted caring for three preschoolers.

At first, I ignored the bedwetting. Perhaps it would stop on its own. When it didn't, I explained to Bill that he was too big a boy to wet the bed. The wetting continued. I reasoned with him, threatened him, shouted at him, and spanked him. The wetting continued. I felt angry and frustrated.

A. S. Neill frequently dealt with problem behavior by rewarding his students. Rewards for bad behavior didn't make sense to me, but nothing else I tried had worked. I was desperate. Neill's ideas had worked with the man at the door. I decided to try them with the bedwetting problem.

The next time Bill wet the bed, I gave him a penny. He stared at me in confusion. The following morning, his bed was dry. He never wet the bed again. My anger and frustration disappeared.

Wow! What a powerful tool! I began using Neill's ideas with neighboring children.

One day, two children were calling each other names in the back yard and threatening to fight. Instead of trying to stop them, I took each aside and asked him if he wanted to fight.

"I don't want to fight," each responded, "but he's making me do it. He's calling me names."

"Do you want to fight?" I reiterated. "If you do, go ahead and do it."

The boys mumbled to themselves and looked at the ground. Two minutes later, they were playing happily together.

What I was doing contradicted everything society had taught me, but it brought the peace and harmony I desired. Society had taught me to punish people for "bad behavior," but I wasn't punishing them. Society had taught me to resist "evil," but I was no longer resisting. Society had taught me to fight for peace, but I wasn't fighting.

Instead, I was simply detaching from the anger and turmoil around me and allowing it to happen without responding to it. The anger and turmoil disappeared, and my life and relationships worked. By allowing myself to remain peaceful and harmonious, everything around me became peaceful and harmonious.

As a child, I had understood Matthew 6:39 as a puzzling and unattainable moral commandment, requiring subservience of my own needs to the needs of others. Suddenly, in a different experiential context, those same words took on an entirely new meaning. They didn't require subservience of my own needs to the needs of others. Rather, they suggested extremely effective action I could take all by myself, that benefited both others and me. There was no self-denial in my actions. There was nothing but self-affirmation and life affirmation. I had never before felt so free, so strong, so powerful, so integrated, so fully in control.

Nothing outside me changed. Only my perceptions, thoughts, actions, and emotions changed.

What I experienced has been called a "mystical experience." It contained all four of the characteristics documented by William

James in his book *The Varieties of Religious Experience:* ineffability (incapable of description), noetic quality (a profound sense of knowing), transiency, and passivity.

I couldn't describe or communicate the deeper meaning.

I somehow just knew that I knew.

The experience happened and passed.

It was not an experience and consciousness shift I chose, although I chose the actions that preceded it.

As a child, I was taught to doubt, question, and trust my own judgment. My rearing didn't include education about mystical experiences, but I knew that many religions contained words describing similar experiences. As I read texts from Christianity, Buddhism, Zen Buddhism, Confucianism, Taoism, Islam, Hinduism, Plato, and existentialist philosophers, I could recognize my own experience in all the different words.

It was as if different people were describing the same beautiful flower garden. Some talked about roses, some spoke of delphiniums, some noticed the color patterns, and some focused on the trellises and paths. If I hadn't seen the flower garden and were just listening to the words, I would have thought the people were talking about different things. Having seen the flower garden, I knew they were all giving verbal structure and form to the same underlying experience, just as our minds give form and meaning to the fixed lines of optical illusions or ink blots.

I couldn't stop playing with these ideas. Was my life the same or was it different? Externally, not a thing had changed. Internally, my life was totally transformed. My perceptions, emotions, and actions had suddenly shifted. Words and their experiential meanings had changed. Suddenly, I was looking at and understanding the externals from a sparkling new perspective.

Did I know or did I know nothing? I wasn't sure. There was a sense in which I absolutely "knew," because I could relate my own experience to other people's words about similar experiences. There was another sense in which I "knew" I knew nothing. There were no correct words with which to communicate what I had experienced.

Religious words are gorgeous art, reflecting this universal underlying transformational experience. Offered as guides, they serve humanity well. Presented as Truth, they become false idols that separate and divide.

The meaning of words depends on the human consciousness that hears and understands them. Words have meaning only in the context of particular experiences and mindsets.

*Words*

Words reflect
unique time
place
experience
perspective

Words jangle
unique time
place
experience
perspective of another
and create fear.

Words mirror
unique time
place
experience
perspective of another
and soothe.

Words clarify
unique time
place
experience
perspective of another

and transform.

# Part Two

# *Words and Meaning*

*Mind*

Monsters created
by machinations of mind
self destruct. Let go.

Mind forms false idols,
creating separation.
Analysis splits.

# 2

# The Law of Polarity

## *Yin and Yang*

We are in the fields of perplexity... Wait awhile, for
perplexity is the beginning of knowledge.

—KAHLIL GIBRAN

WE ALL KNOW ABOUT the law of polarity. Each thing is understood only in relation to its opposite: black in relation to white,
tall in relation to short, good in relation to evil.

Remember the Genesis story of the Garden of Eden?

God told Adam and Eve they could eat anything in the garden, except the fruit of the Tree of Knowledge. When they dis-
obeyed God, they suddenly realized they were naked and they
suddenly became ashamed. Absolutely nothing changed about
Adam and Eve except the way they perceived themselves and
their environment. Before, they had been one with God. Now
they were separate and apart from God. If they hadn't eaten of
the Tree of Knowledge, the concepts naked and ashamed would
have meant nothing. Because they ate of the Tree of Knowledge,
these concepts suddenly became divisive.

What does this story mean in relation to language?

Doesn't language separate and divide? Can the concept naked have any meaning except in relation to the concept clothed? Can the concept ashamed have any meaning except in relation to the concept unashamed? If it weren't for language, wouldn't we simply be experiencing sensations and feelings? Before Adam and Eve ate of the fruit of the Tree of Knowledge, weren't they simply experiencing sensations and feelings?

If I were to ask you to describe the color black, without reference to anything else, how would you describe it? As a void? As an absence of light? What do these phrases mean?

Difficult, isn't it?

But if you were allowed to describe black by pointing to a black umbrella, a black flashlight, a black shirt, pretty soon I'd get the idea of what black meant. Maybe you'd turn out all the lights in a dark room at night. This is a different idea of black. Which is the real meaning of black? Aren't all these concepts created? Aren't they all taught?

Remember the story of the Tower of Babel? Perhaps, it should have been called the Tower of Babble.

The Babylonians decided to build a tower to reach God. When God learned about it, He confused their speech, so they couldn't understand one another. Then, God scattered them throughout the earth.

Our speech is still confused. In the Biblical Book of Revelation, it is Babylon, symbolic of our confused speech, that is ultimately judged and burned with fire. (Rev. 18:2, et seq.)

Aren't the words black and white, tall and short, good and evil created by the human mind? Aren't these opposite words simply tools for approximate communication?

Is a man whose height is 5'8", tall or short? Doesn't the answer depend on whether he is standing next to a man whose height is 6'2" or a man whose height is 4'10"? Aren't all words relative?

God is the Creator. Man is created in the image of his Maker. Is man also a creator—of words—of images—of environments—of hate—of love?

Think of the implications of this.

If we humans are creators, each of us has unlimited free choice. Is that a soothing or a frightening thought?

If I have free choice, that's soothing. It's also overwhelming. I've got a lot of responsibility.

If you have free choice, that's scary. You might not do what I want you to do.

It's also humbling. I'd better treat you well, because I may need your help and cooperation.

Eating of the fruit of the Tree of Knowledge—creating opposite words from the whole cloth of experience—caused man's exile from the symbolic Garden of Eden. Can words be catalysts for a return to that Garden of Eden, a return to reunification with that non-dual consciousness that some have called God?

*Awakening*

Today, I listen,
hear it for the first time—

a cardinal greeting the sun.

And then, as I release all thoughts
of yesterday, tomorrow,
spring suddenly surrounds me

and I am.

## Babylon

First came the experience
Then came the word.
The word conveyed the experience
Or did it?
Perhaps, it only pointed.

First came experiences
then came words,
The words divided and distorted.
We listened to the words, and
we, too, became divided and distorted.
Good fought with evil,
knowledge with ignorance,
truth with falsehood,
science with religion.

Each man chose word weapons,
hurling his words against others
dividing,
distorting.

The words fought and contradicted
and we fought and contradicted.
Each word wanted to reign supreme, and
each man wanted to reign supreme.

# 3

# Optical Illusions

*Perception and Belief*

O Arjuna behold in one place the entire universe,
both dynamic and static, and also whatever you
wish to see further. —THE BHAGAVAD GITA

LOOK AT THE FAMOUS optical illusion on the opposite page.
What do you see?

The lines on the paper are fixed, final, and unchanging.
However, your mind organizes these lines into a picture with
meaning. The meaning your mind gives to the lines shifts as
your perception shifts. As your perception shifts, your words
and emotions shift.

The words in this book are fixed, final, and unchanging.
However, your mind gives meaning to these words based on
your past experiences and personal conditioning. New experiences can shift the meaning your mind gives to these words,
simultaneously shifting your emotions and actions. Wouldn't
you like to shift your fear to courage, your anger to inner peace,
your self-righteousness to acceptance? Wouldn't you like to
learn how to shift your perceptions, words and actions so that

your relationships are always warm, mutually supportive, and peaceful? Keep reading.

Our entire world is just like an optical illusion. Our sensory data is fixed, final, and unchanging. Our minds chop it up into separate parts, label it with words, and give it meaning. Sometimes, we chop it up and label it the same way. Most of us looking at a daffodil would agree we were looking at a yellow flower.

Sometimes, however, we chop our sensory data up differently and label it differently. John sees a charming and beautiful young woman. John's wife sees a flirting bitch. Which of them is right?

Buddhists speak of piercing the veil of illusion. Suddenly we become aware that our minds are shaping sensory data and we realize we have a choice as to how we shape it.

What did you see in the optical illusion? Did you see an old hag or a beautiful young woman? Which do you prefer to see?

# 4

# Ink Blots and Cloud Patterns

## *Creating Meaning*

It's not what you look at that matters, it's what
you see.                    —HENRY DAVID THOREAU

INK BLOTS AND CLOUD patterns are similar to optical illusions. Our senses absorb what is "out there." Our minds creatively organize this "stuff" into lines, colors, and shapes and
then give meaning to the lines, colors, and shapes, and label
the parts with words. The words and meanings shift from individual to individual, depending on each person's conditioning,
past experiences, and focus.

Look at the ink blot at the top of Plate I (*inside front cover*).
How many figures can you see? Write down everything you see,
whether large or small. Now pick one shape you see and write a
sentence or two about it. Would those words be true about the
other shapes you listed?

Look at the cloud patterns at the bottom of Plate I. What do
you see? Make a list of every figure you notice. Pick one of the
figures and write a few sentences about it. If you see the polar
bear in the upper left portion of the picture, and your friend
sees the two figures talking in the middle left, do you think your

19

words will be the same? Do you think you will be able to communicate meaningfully? Is it possible you would even argue about what the cloud patterns really show?

Our world is just like these ink blots and cloud patterns. Start looking—really looking—at the sensory data around you. Don't label it the way you've been taught. In fact, for just a moment, don't label it at all. Just notice. Let it flood into your being. You may see things you never saw before. You may find new words flooding into your mind from sources you can't identify. This noticing, or awareness, is the source of all great religious words, poetry, science, and art.

## Form and Substance

Life spirit—infinite energy—
dies, transforms, rebirths
into new creation.

*Haiku*

Words twist and distort
the perfect imperfection.
Wholeness divided.

# 5

# Words and Experience

## *Connection and Context*

Every word is a preconceived judgment.

—WILHELM FRIEDRICH NIETZSCHE

WORDS DIVIDE. EXPERIENCE DOESN'T. A beautiful sunset just is. A hug just is.

As soon as we describe the sunset, we chop 'being' into some of its reflected parts—some of its facets—those facets we happen to be focusing on in that moment. We may label it magnificent or peaceful, orange or rose. Does this mean it is not red or pink or glorious?

Transformed consciousness is nothing more than the direct, non-dual experience of our own ink blot, the immediacy of our own sensory awareness, the sudden understanding of the experiential meaning of another's words, and the sudden realization that we, too, are creators.

Words that describe our experiences are tricky. With a single change in a single word, the whole focus and meaning of a conversation shifts.

Once, I asked a friend whether she was willing to release beliefs that didn't serve her. She answered yes, but changed my word release to discard. I hadn't asked her if she was willing to discard beliefs. I never discard beliefs. Every belief or assumption I've ever had has been valid from a particular perspective at a particular time. Every religious doctrine is valid from a particular perspective at a particular time. Every scientific theory is valid from a particular perspective at a particular time. When I used the word release, I was referring to a process where I choose my focus—the word, thought, or belief that will serve me best in the moment.

Some words imprison. Others free. I always try to choose freeing words and release the imprisoning ones. I'd suggest you do the same. You'll be far happier.

We all have sensory data impinging on our eyes, ears, noses, tongues, and touch—like the optical illusions, ink blots, and cloud patterns. Each of us, through our minds and language, organizes this raw sensory data into meaningful form and gives it labels: ocean, blue, salty. With some sensory data, we all seem to organize it the same way and agree on the same labels. We all call a flat, rectangular surface, supported by four legs, a table. We all call a lilac a lavender flower.

But what happens when we start using more abstract labels like right, wrong, truth, falsehood, knowledge, ignorance, God, Devil, heaven, hell? Can we agree on what these mean by looking at the raw data impinging on our senses? Can we structure the ink blot of experience into a meaningful form that separates right from wrong, truth from falsehood, knowledge from ignorance, God from Devil, heaven from hell?

Why have we fought bloody battles for centuries over right, truth, God, and Heaven? Because words divide and we often allow them to divide us. We allow them to pit one person against another in a fear-ridden, power struggle. We label ourselves good and the other person evil.

Suppose you were to spend a week in Honduras and I had never been there. You return and tell me about passion fruit, monkeylalas, and sergeant majors. How much will I understand? Will I picture the monkeys I've seen in the San Diego Zoo when you were talking about funny looking lizards? Will I picture armed men in uniforms when you were talking about reef fish? Will I really know what a monkeylala is until I see one or at least see a picture of one?

Suppose I were so impressed with your description of monkeylalas, that I borrowed some of your word labels, added my personal experiences with monkeys in the San Diego Zoo, and began talking to other people about monkeylalas. Would I know what I was talking about? Wouldn't I simply be manipulating your word labels without any direct experience of my own?

When you were talking about monkeylalas, did I hear what you meant to say? Of course not! I heard your words, translated into my own personal experiences.

If I were to travel to Honduras and experience a monkeylala for myself, my experience would have a depth your words didn't have. Maybe I'd say, "Oh, now I understand what a monkeylala is." Or, "I didn't picture them running along on their hind legs." Or, "Oh my gosh! These aren't at all like what I saw in the San Diego Zoo."

After I saw for myself what a monkeylala was, wouldn't your words take on a different meaning? Wouldn't I now have a better understanding of what they meant? Wouldn't our experiences of monkeylalas have a similarity that would enable us to talk meaningfully about monkeylalas?

I might even be tempted to say that your words about monkeylalas were true, even though you didn't mention that monkeylalas ran along on their hind legs. I would recognize the words you used to describe your experience of monkeylalas in terms of my own experience.

Would the words you had chosen be the only true words for that monkeylala experience? Of course not! Each person who experienced a monkeylala would describe it differently. Which are the True words? All of them because they adequately describe the experience, or none of them, because each set of words is only a partial, creative description?

Suppose both John and Mary had been to Honduras and seen monkeylalas. I had never been there. If I were just listening to their words about monkeylalas, I might decide that John's words were right and Mary's words were wrong. I would be hearing only the differences in the words, without being able to relate those word differences to the underlying experience of a monkeylala. I might even assume that because the words were different, the underlying experiences were different.

What would make me decide that John's words were right, and Mary's words were wrong? Am I afraid of John? Has John been kinder to me than Mary? Do I need something John can give me that Mary can't?

Verbal communication is something like playing that old game, Whisper Down the Lane or Telephone. The first person whispers something in the ear of the second, the second whispers what he heard in the ear of the third. By the time the words reach the last person in line, they are totally distorted.

When we worship words, we worship false idols. To the extent that words are perceived as True, rather than simply as symbols that point to one person's perception of an experience, they are false idols. For example, two different people could touch a hotplate. One might insist it is burning hot. The other might insist, "It's not that hot." Each statement is a statement about one person's individual perception. Neither is a statement about the actual temperature of the hotplate.

Nevertheless, both individuals could easily insist that their own words were true, because that's the way each has mentally and emotionally structured his or her unique experience. They could even argue over who was right and who was wrong. Opposite words can and do describe identical experiences.

None of this means that we can't use words to focus our minds and bring our lives into harmony. This is what good religion and good spirituality do. They are a means to an end, not an end in themselves.

Is it possible that identical words can be either true or false, depending on who uses them, how they are used, what they mean in terms of experience, and whether they emanate directly from the ground of being, ink blot of experience, substance underlying form, God, universal energy, or whatever other label we choose for that which underlies human words and is indescribable?

Words like God, heaven, and eternity do have meaning in relation to certain kinds of human experiences and certain ways of thinking about those experiences. All those words are efforts to communicate an altered state of consciousness, a changed way of thinking, an internal change, an individual mental shift, an individual emotional shift, an individual conduct change.

They are efforts to distinguish a prior human consciousness, understood through words like Devil, hell, and time, from a new, non-dual, creative, and transformed state of consciousness, understood through words like God, heaven, and eternity.

Each of us is like the mustard seed, needing only fertile ground and nurturing to grow into a magnificent plant. Can each of us nurture this seed in ourselves and others until we grow into a magnificent plant? Together, can we grow into that great human garden of love, tolerance, and harmony? Is this what is meant by a return to the Garden of Eden?

## The Fall

In the beginning
the earth was without form and void, and
darkness was upon the face of the deep.

Then man's senses experienced
dividing light from dark
and man's mind created words
"light" and "darkness"
and man moralized
that light was good and
darkness was evil.

Man saw the brilliant scarlet of the poppies
and created red.
He felt the warmth of the sun
and created security and comfort.
He experienced the anguish of death
and created grief.
He experienced pain and created the Devil.
He experienced serenity
and created God.

Then man became enamored of his creations
exalting them into moral doctrines.
Pain was bad and serenity was good.
The Devil was bad and God was good.
Man posed as God
proclaiming his word creations right
and other word creations wrong.

Each man created his own tree of knowledge
of good and evil
and each man believed that
his tree of knowledge was
The Tree of Knowledge
applicable to all.

An occasional man extracted himself
from the human creations and word idols
into which he was born
and returned to the experience
from which they evolved.

Men who still worshipped word idols
pronounced him
"saint," "savior," or "devil."
Freeing himself from the word shackles
binding humanity
he returned to the experience
from which all arose.

Free to experience the beauty of the poppies.
Free to experience the warmth of the sun.
Free to experience the pain and joy of human existence.
Free to use mind to create
in the image of his Maker.

Experiencing
through cleansed eyes
he created fresh word forms
glowing with honesty

Human words.
Individualized words.
Unique words.
Pure words.

Men who still worshipped false idols
parroted the pure words
desecrating them into false idols.

From the mouths of idolators
the pure words became profanity.
From the mouths of idolators,
the pure words became instruments of control.
From the mouths of idolators,
the pure words became the opposite
of what saviors and saints intended.
From the mouths of idolators,
the pure words became shackles to bind mankind
rather than tools to free him.

Author's note: If language is an instrument of mind, how does one use divisional language to synthesize? How does one become whole through separation?

This being a place of words, it seems appropriate
to speak of them. They are, in essence, among the
magician's most primary of tools, creating bridges
between the unreal and the unreal, and in the
process, creating reality.

Like arrows dipped in poison or soft cloths
dipped in healing balm and applied to a forehead,
they are the transport system of essence. And, yet,
like most else in life, we often take them for granted,
blinded to their deeper magic. There is a place of
standing where the most potent crystal is merely
a rock, where the most sacred place, merely real
estate. And like the Sorcerer's Apprentice, we often
fiddle around with our words blindly, unaware of
the effects that easily rage out of control. Yet it is
from words that reality proceeds and it is by words
that it is molded and changed.      —JAE MALONE

# PART THREE

## *Words as Dualistic Dividers*

*Haiku*

Spikes we call knowledge
ruthlessly crucify our
creativity.

# 6

# Ignorance and Knowledge

## In What Ways Can We Know?

> A knowledge of our own ignorance is the first step
> toward true knowledge.　　　　　—Socrates

A cook, an artist, and a physicist were all looking at the same rectangular surface. The cook saw a table on which he could chop onions, parsley, and carrots. The artist saw a series of colors that he could reproduce on canvas. The physicist saw electrons, protons, and neutrons spinning in space. Which one had knowledge? Which was ignorant? Who was right? Who was wrong?

If we want a delicious bowl of vegetable soup for lunch, perhaps we can say that the cook knows what the rectangular surface is: a place to chop vegetables. Clearly, neither a series of colors nor atoms spinning in space is going to get us that bowl of soup.

If we want a lovely picture to decorate our living room wall, it is the artist who knows, with his series of colors to be reproduced on canvas. Chopping onions, parsley, and carrots won't get us the painting, nor will spinning electrons, protons, and neutrons.

If the cook, artist, and physicist all agree to call the rectangular surface "a table" or *une table* or *una mesa*, could we say that they know what the rectangular surface is? If all Europeans in the fourteenth century agreed that the earth was flat, could we say that they knew the earth was flat? Could we say that the earth really is flat? I don't think so.

What is this thing called knowledge anyway? What is this thing called ignorance? Can we know anything with one hundred percent certainty?

Sensory data is sensory data. We all chop it up into words all the time, and we all do it differently—just like the cook, the artist, and the physicist.

Each human mind creatively separates one portion of our sensory data from another; remembers, analyzes, divides, structures and restructures it to create patterns with which each self can be comfortable. Can we agree, through mutual respect, to create patterns with which all of us can be comfortable, patterns we can agree to call knowledge, even if just for limited purposes? Is this what scientists mean by hypothesis and theory?

## Scylla and Charybdis

Enmeshed in the web of imperfection,
silence denies my purpose;
speaking distorts.

Absurd and foolish is my speech,
yet speak I must.

Answers have I not,
but only an awareness.

## Questions

"There are no wrong questions," he said
with certainty in his voice.
"There are only wrong answers."

Perhaps

But

If I ask a meaningless question,
can I expect a meaningful answer?

If I ask an ambiguous question,
can I expect a clear answer?

For are not question and answer
corollaries of a single idea?
and does not the right answer
lie in the right question?

# 7

# Falsehood and Truth

## *Putting the Puzzle Together*

For words divide and rend;
But silence is most noble till the end.

—ALGERNON CHARLES SWINBURNE

WE ALL TAKE WHAT'S out there, chop it up, and label the parts with words. We see what we want to see and chop it up the way we need to chop it up to protect ourselves.

Then, we get attached to our own words and argue with people whose word labels are different or people who chop reality up differently from the way we chop it up. Sometimes, we even become angry because other people don't agree with our word labels.

We all believe in illusions—word illusions. I call them word sculptures. We have to believe in something, but if we're going to believe in something, why not make it a conscious decision instead of a knee-jerk reaction?

Your words are always true for you, because of the way you structure your reality. In how many different ways can you structure that reality? Which ways do you like best?

39

At the same time, your words may not be true for others, who structure their reality differently. If you truly want to communicate, make sure you know what John means when he talks about the beach. Is he talking about Waikiki or Atlantic City? There's a huge experiential difference between the two. If he's talking about Waikiki, and you're thinking Atlantic City, it's likely that you're not going to hear what he's saying.

Make sure you are clear about what you want to say before you open your mouth. Which ways of chopping up reality are likely to get you the results you want? Do you want to say, "You're a no-good slob. I hate you." Or do you want to say, "I love you, but I don't like it when you throw your underwear on the floor. Would you mind picking it up?" Do you want to end your relationship or do you want the underwear off the floor?

This book is an illusion. It is written using word art—my own choices in chopping up reality. You will either like the words I choose or you won't. If you don't like my words, please sculpt your own. They will likely serve you better than borrowing mine. There is only one rule: use your words in ways that serve yourself, others, and our planet, not in ways that harm.

John and Joan are putting together a puzzle. They separate out the edge pieces, and, by trial and error, put them together to form a rectangle. Then they start sorting the remaining pieces by color: blue shades here, red shades there, yellow shades over there. Working with similar pieces, they begin to form larger patterns where the pieces all fit. Eventually, the entire puzzle is done, each piece in its own place, all nicely fitting together as part of the whole.

Can John and Joan say it's true they finished the puzzle and got everything right? Can they say they have the answer? They understand exactly how that puzzle is put together. They could do it again. They could teach others how to do it. Other people could do it separately and end up with the same result.

While John and Joan may know how to put together that particular puzzle, do they know anything outside the borders of the puzzle?

No. They have only completed the one puzzle with which they are working—by solving internal relationships until the puzzle is whole.

There *is* a Human Truth Puzzle that can be put together over and over by person after person so that every piece fits, exactly the way a jigsaw puzzle can be put together over and over. Many have done it throughout the ages: Jesus, the Buddha, Lao Tzu, Socrates, Plato, Mohammed, Martin Luther King, Jr., Gandhi, Zen masters, Hermann Hesse, Kahlil Gibran, Friedrich Wilhelm Nietzsche, William Shakespeare, Pablo Picasso, Walt Whitman, Ernest Holmes, to name a few. We 'know' we've figured out this same Human Truth Puzzle because there's a resonance between our thoughts, words, feelings, and actions and the thoughts, words, feelings and actions of those who've gone before us. All the pieces of the puzzle fit.

Teaching others how to put the puzzle together, however, challenges the most creative master, because three of the puzzle variables are human perception, human words, and the human mind.

How does one use divisive, analytic words to assemble a holistic, non-dual experience and perspective? How can one communicate meaning when a single word means something different, experientially, to each human mind that hears it?

What creative tools have the masters used to communicate their wisdom about how the Human Truth Puzzle fits together, and how that wisdom can be used to serve every person on this planet?

Most have used some form of word art:

Poetry (Kahlil Gibran)

Parables (Jesus)

Questions (Socrates)

Novels (Hermann Hesse)

Commandments (Moses)

Some have used silence or meditation (Buddhist monks), and a few have used odd kinds of mind-bending puzzles, like koans (Zen Buddhist monks).

When we try to move beyond the edges of the Human Truth Puzzle, we can't know. We simply have to trust. That's what a leap of faith is all about. We leap beyond our linear thinking, our divisive language, and our fear of the unknown to free our creativity.

We all have the ability to put this Human Truth Puzzle together, but it's not easy. Who is up to the challenge of looking hard at his own thoughts, emotions, and actions? Who is willing to explore the emotional depths of her own terror, so that she can move through that hell to the psychological heaven on the other side? "Narrow is the way, which leadeth unto life, and few there be that find it." (Matt. 7:14)

Words can point to Truth, but words are not Truth. This Human Truth Puzzle can only be experienced—as synthesis, peace, harmony, and unity. As soon as we label the experience of non-dual consciousness Truth, the mind jumps in and opposes Truth to Falsehood. The human mind has then created the very duality the unification experience dispels.

Just like the completed Human Truth Puzzle, there are some word sculptures that can properly be labeled reflections of what has been called Truth and others that can be considered distortions of what has been called Truth. Word sculptures that reflect what has been called Truth are carefully selected to empower each individual and maximize harmony on this planet. They catalyze an optimum interaction of dynamic, unique human beings. They emanate from a conscious awareness of how words work, how our minds work, and choices we have available.

There is a human map that can be comprehended. There is a Human Truth Puzzle that can be completed, over and over again by person after person. It cannot be mapped by words. It can only be experienced.

Comprehending the Human Truth Puzzle is not an outside job. It requires understanding one's own mind, emotions, and consciousness. Delving deep into one's own consciousness is a terrifying and humbling experience. How many of us are willing to undertake the journey?

Solving the Human Truth Puzzle requires a conscious awareness of the relationship between our experiences and the words we use to chop them up: knowledge/ignorance; black/white; right/wrong. One facet of conscious awareness is selecting words that create harmony rather than discord. This is the only viable choice for a consciousness that has delved deep into its own hellish caverns. Any other alternative is far too destructive and terrifying.

Another facet of conscious awareness is understanding and being connected to the core energy and dynamics to which any words are attached. Words uttered by one who is consciously aware will be Truth from his lips. The same words, uttered by one who is not consciously aware will be lies—the parroting of someone else's words when the speaker has no personal, experiential understanding.

There is no linguistic truth other than the linguistic truth men create and agree upon. There is no knowledge other than the knowledge all men agree to call knowledge. There is no right or wrong other than the concepts of right and wrong men have created.

Is it possible that there could be a God outside the boundaries of the Human Truth Puzzle? If all man can know is the constant influx of sensory data and his mind's structuring of that data, he can never know whether there really is a God. He can only believe and trust. If he chooses to believe and trust, he does so only because that is what brings peace and harmony to himself and others.

There are many humans throughout history, who have plunged deep into the depths of their own personal hells and emerged experiencing this constant awareness of the influx of sensory data and their own mind's creative structuring of that data. Many have labeled their resurrection from dualistic words salvation or piercing the veil of illusion or transformation, and their human, non-dual consciousness heaven or nirvana. All feel somehow connected to an Energy far greater than their own, an Energy many have called God. Many of those same humans, when looking back on their previous lack of awareness and imprisonment behind the rigid bars of language and fear, have labeled their previous mental and emotional state hell. Can the words God and Devil have experiential meaning within the framework of the Human Truth Puzzle, within human experience, and within the mind's creative structuring of that experience, just as the words blue and ocean have meaning within that framework? Is it no wonder that mystics cannot describe the God they experience? Is it no wonder that the human experience that has been called God is described as omniscient, omnipotent and omnipresent, yet at the same time humbling and terrifying? It includes every nuance, every possibility.

44

## *Haiku Couplets (If)*

Thought starts with premise
How can man then think thought is
universal truth?

Thought starts with premise
is not thought naught but Godlike
creativity?

## Rules

Man's rules of right and wrong
Brew bitter fights in

court
battlefield
street
home

consuming

court
battlefield
street
home

with

tension
fear
anger
frustration

God has no rules of right and wrong

God only releases

tension
      fear
            anger
                  frustration

to free

love
      acceptance
             respect
                creativity

## *Helpful (Not Right) Rules*

DO:

1. Trust yourself.
2. Learn about yourself.
3. Be honest with yourself.
4. Ask yourself:
    a. What do I think?
    b. What do I feel?
    c. What do I need?
    d. What are my choices?
5. Love yourself.
6. Do whatever you want as long as you aren't hurting anyone, including yourself.
7. Make your own decisions.
8. Take care of yourself.
9. Share yourself with others.
10. Hug.

DON'T:

1. Focus on other people.
2. Focus on theories or doctrines.
3. Hurt other people.
4. Judge other people.
5. Control other people.

# 8

# Evil and Good
# (Wrong and Right)

## *Changing the Function of Dysfunctional Words*

No law can be sacred to me but that of my
nature. Good and bad are but names very readily
transferable to that or this; the only right is what is
after my own constitution; the only wrong what is
against it. —RALPH WALDO EMERSON

I DON'T LIKE THE words evil and good. They smack of judgment.
Why not use the words functional and dysfunctional instead?

Suppose you buy a brand new BMW? The tires are inflated
to exactly thirty-two pounds. The seats are adjustable to exactly
the right position for a long, comfortable drive. The battery is
properly hooked up to the starter, junction block, and alterna-
tor, so that the engine starts at the turn of the key. The gas tank
is full of premium gasoline, and that car rolls.

Now suppose you buy the same BMW, but the tires are inflated to only twenty pounds. Nothing happens when you pull
the lever to adjust the seat. When you sit in the driver's seat, it
feels stiff and too low to see the road clearly. Someone forgot to

attach the battery cables to the starter. When you turn the key, nothing happens. The gas tank is empty. The car doesn't move. It can't perform its proper function of transporting you from home to office.

Would we say that the first car is good and the second car, evil? No. We would say that the first car works and is functional, and the second car doesn't work and is dysfunctional.

Moreover, the first car is functional only for a particular purpose, transporting us from one place to another. If we need to landscape a beautiful garden, both cars would be dysfunctional.

You and I are just like those two cars.

We can drink clean, filtered water. We can eat fresh, organic fruits and vegetables. We can walk a mile a day. We can keep our focus on what we need to change in ourselves, not on what others need to change. We're not good for doing this. We're just more functional.

We can drink chlorinated tap water or soda, eat pesticide-sprayed fruits and vegetables, sit around watching TV, sleep on a lumpy mattress with blankets that leave us too warm or too cold, focus on what others ought to change instead of what we need to change in ourselves. We're not evil for doing this. We're just less functional.

Do you want to be more functional or less functional?

For the BMW to be functional, each part, by itself, must be functional. The battery must work. The starter must work. There must be gas in the tank. The seat must be the proper height. But beyond that, all parts must work harmoniously together. All parts working together results in a superb machine that does exactly what we want it to do.

You and I are the same way. Our hearts must be working, our lungs must be working, our joints and muscles must be working, and most of all, our minds must be working. When all these parts work harmoniously together, they produce an energized, joyful, positive, effective person.

What about the larger community?

Suppose you are caring for yourself, and I am not. You are happy, energetic, and functional. I am sad, lethargic, and marginally functional. You offer me clean water, and I snap back that I like soda. You offer me an organic apple, and I tell you I prefer fries. I begin feeling angry over your attempts to control me and tell you to bug off. You feel hurt when you were only trying to help, even though you respect my right to make my own choices. How will you handle it? Will you back off from me, spend less time with me, look for other relationships? Will I lose a good friend?

Are you good and am I evil?

No. You are functional and I am dysfunctional. Because I am dysfunctional, our relationship doesn't work smoothly. We are unable to create exciting things together.

Does it benefit you for me to be dysfunctional? Absolutely not. It benefits you for me to be functional.

Expand this analogy to millions of people. Some take care of themselves and are positive, energetic, and joyful. Others don't or don't know how. Those who take care of themselves are flexible, open-minded, and supportive, and create a dynamic heaven on earth. Those who don't or don't know how create a living hell.

A friend recently asked, "Are genocide and the holocaust just unwise choices or are they evil? What about a willful choice to harm another human? Isn't that evil?

These are terrific questions!

We can certainly label genocide, the Holocaust, and a willful choice to harm another human evil. Churches have been doing this for years. I'd rather think of people who commit genocide or support holocausts as extremely dysfunctional people. They have never learned how to care for themselves. How can one expect them to care for others? They certainly create a living hell through their ignorance, not only for the people they persecute, but for themselves as well.

The only reason I don't like the words wrong and evil is because they're divisive. They encourage judgment and conflict. For example, if I think I'm right and you're wrong, I'm judging you. That is not my job. My job is to keep my own steps as straight as I can. If I think you're wrong, I may also try to force you to do things the right way—my way. Force never resolves anything. Only love and respect do.

Certainly, genocide and holocausts are unwise choices if what we want to create is a peaceful, prosperous planet where humans respect one another and work together in harmony. Yes, we can label them evil if we want, but what do we accomplish? Doesn't this just beget pride in us and guilt in others? We, of course, would never do such a horrible thing, but then we have never walked in those other shoes. Pride and guilt divide and cripple. We serve neither ourselves nor others by using the words good and evil.

What is my responsibility to myself, to you, to the larger society? First, to care for myself, so that I am positive, energetic, joyful, and functional. Second, to support you in your efforts to be functional. Third, to brainstorm, mastermind, and take action with other positive, energetic, joyful people to create a living, breathing, dynamic, loving, expanding heaven on earth.

## Master Sculptor

We, blessed with
mind, choice, language,
struggle to shape
eternity
to our wills.

Against it, we hurl
our finite selves
straining.

To no avail.

The Sculptor,
silent,
watches

as we chip away our follies
against the immovable void
until perfected

we acquiesce

in defeat
in mastery
in harmony

## Limitation

When man defines God,
god is no longer God

# 9

# Devil and God

## *Dysfunctional and Functional Energies*

And thus I clothe my naked villany
With odd old ends stol'n forth of holy writ,
And seem a saint when most I play the devil.

—WILLIAM SHAKESPEARE

DID YOU NOTICE THE similarity between the words devil and evil? Between the words God and good?

None of the world religions has ever been able to define God. God is referred to as a mystery, something beyond human understanding. The word define means to limit. Of course, religions can't define God. What right do we humans have to limit God?

If we think of God as undifferentiated energy that manifests in infinite differentiated forms, aren't we presumptuous if we try to limit the form that energy may take? Aren't we imprisoning human creativity and manifestation by imposing arbitrary human rules and structures on that creativity and manifestation? Aren't we defying God by trying to force all human activity into a single mold, by standardizing behavior and limiting emotion?

Perhaps the energy that some have called God did not intend you to be exactly like me. Perhaps you are intended to become who you are so that you and I may enrich one another.

# 10

# Hell and Heaven

## A State of Consciousness

The kingdom of God is within you.

—LUKE 17:21

HAS THE KINGDOM OF Heaven always been a creative possibility here on earth? Has Eternity always been present in time? What if the only reason we have not experienced Heaven and Eternity is because we have not permitted ourselves to tune in and align ourselves with their creative energy and power?

As fallible human beings, we have been powerless to remove blinders we didn't know we were wearing. We have been incapable of releasing our subconscious fears of inadequacy. We have been unable to stand tall in the face of each other's human ridicule and accept our personal uniqueness.

Are the Kingdom of Heaven and Eternity universal states of consciousness attainable by every human? Is it possible that the Kingdom of Heaven and Eternity will actualize when every human is open and consciously attuned to their energy and power?

Heaven and hell are not physical places where we go after our bodies die. They are states of consciousness right here, right now, on this planet. Salvation is not physical ascension into the clouds after our bodies die, playing harps, never having to work, and having all our needs met. It is a sudden expansion of consciousness now, a sudden mental restructuring of our sensory data so that we no longer perceive it as threatening, but simply as there, to be creatively and peacefully structured.

This experience/perspective called Heaven in Christian tradition or Nirvana in Buddhist tradition is simply non-dual human consciousness, fully creative and aware.

# 11

# Skepticism and Faith

## The Twin Brothers

Skepticism is the beginning of faith.

—OSCAR WILDE

WHAT IS SKEPTICISM?

Am I skeptical when I watch the sun setting over a peaceful bay? Am I skeptical when I hike a narrow, woodland trail, listening to the sparrows cheep and watching the squirrels scampering along pine boughs? Am I skeptical when I look into the laughing eyes of my two-year-old granddaughter?

No. I am skeptical of human words. I should be skeptical of human words.

Larry promises me that if I buy his tonic, my arthritis will disappear. I buy his tonic. I still have arthritis.

John promises to meet me at Dino's Thursday at 10 a.m. I am there at 10 a.m. John arrives at 10:20.

Monica promises to bring a dish of lasagna to a church buffet dinner. Instead, she brings cheesecake.

Yes, I am skeptical of human words.

A friend of mine is addicted to cocaine. He has no food, because he has spent all his money on drugs. He begs me for money to buy food. I deprive myself of food and give him money. He spends it on more cocaine. Yes, I am skeptical of human words.

What is faith?

Faith is not knowledge. Faith is a choice.

We all believe in something. Scientists believe in theory, experimentation, data, and rational analysis. Most churchgoers believe in God. Whatever you choose to believe in, make it a conscious choice, based on your own thinking and experience.

Here are some other beliefs about belief:

Man is made by his belief. As he believes, so he is.
—THE BHAGAVAD GITA

The faith that stands on authority is not faith.
—RALPH WALDO EMERSON

Be not afraid of life.
Believe that life is worth living and your belief will help create the fact.　　—WILLIAM JAMES

I can tell you, honest friend, what to believe: believe life; it teaches better than book or orator.
—GOETHE

… cling to Faith beyond the forms of Faith.
—ALFRED, LORD TENNYSON

Faith is to believe what we do not see; and the reward of this faith is to see what we believe.
—ST. AUGUSTINE

Faith keeps many doubts in her pay. If I could not doubt, I should not believe.

—Henry David Thoreau

Doubt is not a pleasant condition, but certainty is absurd.

—Voltaire

Faith begins where reason sinks exhausted.

—Albert Pike

Faith-belief is the organ by which we apprehend what is beyond our knowledge. —William Hamilton

Pin your faith to no one's sleeves, haven't you two eyes of your own? —Thomas Carlyle

I conjure you, my brethren, to remain faithful to earth, and do not believe those who speak unto you of superterrestrial hopes! Poisoners they are, whether they know it or not.

—Friedrich Wilhelm Nietzsche

I had to set limits to knowledge in order to make place for faith. —Immanuel Kant

I have great faith in fools; self-confidence my friends call it. —Edgar Allan Poe

If you think you can win, you can win. Faith is necessary to victory. —William Hazlitt

In actual life every great enterprise begins with and takes its first forward step in faith.

—FRIEDRICH VON SCHLEGEL

Painting is a faith, and it imposes the duty to disregard public opinion.     —VINCENT VAN GOGH

What do you choose to believe? Why have you made that choice? What do you gain by holding that belief? What do you lose? Make sure the choice is your own and not implanted by someone else.

# 12

# End and Beginning

## *The Symmetry of Eternity*

I am Alpha and Omega, the beginning and the end,
the first and the last.                     —REV. 22:13

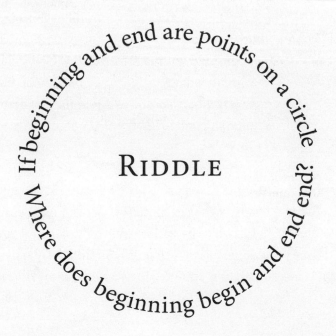

RIDDLE

If beginning and end are points on a circle Where does beginning begin and end end?

# PERSPECTIVE

**DEATH**
Do not mourn death
for without it you
cannot grow to your
fullest height.

**REBIRTH**
Do not mourn death
for without it you
cannot grow to your
fullest height.

**DEATH**
Mourn death, then
transform the en-
ergy of your grief to
new creation.

**REBIRTH**
Mourn death, then
transform the en-
ergy of your grief to
new creation.

# 13

# Death and Life

## *Metamorphosis*

From the death of the old the new proceeds,
And the life of truth from the death of creeds.

—John Greenleaf Whittier

Someday, our bodies will die. Is it possible that our bodies are only a temporary physical abode we inhabit during our days on this earth?

Is it possible that everything, including our bodies, is energy? Could energy remain constant, but the form it takes change? What if the energy that is you and the energy that is I is all part of the same energy manifesting in different forms?

Think of water. When it is very cold, it takes the form of solid ice. When it is very hot, it takes the form of vapor, dissipating into thin air. The rest of the time, it is liquid. This single energy manifests in different ways. So does the energy of our bodies, minds, and spirits.

Your energy and my energy are nurtured from many sources: plants, animals, sun, rain, wind. When our bodies die, they go on to nurture other forms of life.

Your thoughts and my thoughts are each a form of this universal energy. They will always be available as possible thoughts in other lives.

My emotions and your emotions will always be present as possible emotions in other lives. My experiences and your experiences will always be possible experiences in other lives. Is there a sense in which we are all part of the past and part of the future along that chronological line we call time? Is there a sense in which we all exist at every point in time, in every other living creature? Is there a sense in which we all have eternal life-now?

Our genes, thoughts, experiences, and emotions will find expression in our sons and daughters, our grandchildren, our great-grandchildren. Are they eternal thoughts, experiences, and emotions, waiting to be captured by anyone who listens—anytime, anywhere? Is this what is meant by the Akashic records? Is it possible we are all part of the same great universal symphony of humanity?

What is it you are willing to die for? Whatever you are willing to die for is what you must live for.

## Co-Creation

When I know myself,
I know others.

When I know my fears,
I understand the fears of others.

When I notice my masks,
I can penetrate the masks of others.

When I forgive myself,
I can forgive others.

The only power I have
Is the power to change myself,
But when I work on what I can
I co-create with my Maker.

*Free Will and Predestination*

Fumbling,
stumbling
past beckoning doors,
we haltingly wonder

which one to open,
which, disregard?

Silently, destiny, unknown, awaits, and
manifests only when all doors are chosen.

# 14

# Predestination and Free Will

*Different Contexts, Different Meanings*

Man is a masterpiece of creation if for no other
reason than that, all the weight of evidence for
determinism notwithstanding, he believes he has
free will.                                 —G. C. LICHTENBERG

FOUR MEN WERE TRAPPED in a raging fire.

The first man screamed in fear and pain.

The second man became angry and cursed the fire.

The third man prayed to God and denied the fire was either
hot or burning his flesh.

The fourth man opened the door and walked out into the
sunshine.

All of these men were predestined to be trapped in a raging
fire. Yet, once trapped, each made a different choice about how
to handle it.

There is no contradiction between free will and predestination. The two concepts simply apply to different aspects of our
experience.

Predestination is the external circumstances that challenge each of us. Free will is the choices we make when confronted with those external circumstances.

As an old Chinese proverb states, there is opportunity in every challenge. There is also challenge in every opportunity.

# 15

# I Ought and I Want

*Freedom, Risk, and Consequences*

Work and play are words used to describe the same
thing under differing conditions.    —MARK TWAIN

I WANT AND I ought are often enmeshed.

If you do what you ought to do, who prescribed your duty?
Was it the church? Your parents? Your teachers? Yourself?

If it was someone other than yourself, do you experience joy
in what you do or is life hard and serious? Do you find yourself
judging others for not living up to your "oughts"?

If you do what you want to do, you soon discover, through
painful experience, that there are some things you need to do,
even if, in the moment, you don't want to do them.

My mother tells a story about her first year teaching elemen-
tary school during the depths of the Depression. One of her students, Rocco, was constantly talking and poking his neighbors.
His antics distracted his classmates and disrupted my mother's
teaching. She decided it was either him or her, and it wasn't going to be her. She ordered him into the cubbyhole under her
desk.

Moments later, the principal walked in. He waddled over to my mother's desk and slowly eased himself into her chair. Rocco hadn't bargained for a big fat belly cutting off his view of the world. Cowering in terror, he squeezed himself back into the farthest corner of the cubbyhole. The principal never discovered him, but Rocco learned the hard way why it's not a good idea to interfere with others' learning.

Like Rocco, after a few painful experiences, you will want to do what you need to do because you will understand why certain choices are better than others.

Consider doing whatever you want in the moment, provided you aren't harming either yourself or others. Be willing to learn from your mistakes. If they're painful enough, you won't repeat them, because you'll understand why they were bad choices. You'll also start thinking about what you could have done differently that would have given you better results.

If you are choosing the goal you most want or are best able to pursue in the moment, you'll discover you're fully focused, involved, and highly motivated. Moreover, you'll have no need to judge others who aren't doing what you're doing.

It's vital to be able to say yes to your mission in life. You won't be able to do that if you don't know what you want.

*Paths*

A principled man
followed the straight, narrow path of discipline.

A free-thinking man
followed the winding path of exploration.

The principled man
stumbled across a roadblock called I can no longer do it.

The free-thinking man
discovered there is a better way.

And together, they joined hands,
setting forth on the path where discipline and freedom merge.

## Haiku

Cat, tensing, twitching,
focused on innocent prey
soon to awaken.

## Reflections

Reflections of reality
twisted and skewed by motion
mirror faithfully
only when motion ceases.

## Haiku

Teacher and student,
both teaching, learning, thriving—
catalytic growth.

# 16

# Non-Action and Action

## *Action through Detachment*

One who sees inaction in action, and action in
inaction, is intelligent among men.

—THE BHAGAVAD GITA

WHEN JESUS WAS CRUCIFIED on the cross, he took no action
to save himself. Perhaps he recognized the futility of fighting
the embedded human fiefdoms. Perhaps, he was simply living a
belief in non-violence. Perhaps he was simply functioning from
a universal human consciousness that perceived his physical
body as a single physical form of an all-encompassing energy
he chose to call God. Perhaps he perceived his murderers simply as another form of that energy—dysfunctional human beings living in their own fear-created world.

Yet Jesus' non-action was the most powerful action he could
have taken. His life and death generated hundreds of religious
traditions with millions of followers.

When Socrates drank the hemlock, he did so voluntarily. He
wasn't willing to postpone drinking the potion when Criton
begged him to do so. When his friends broke forth in loud lam-
entation as he slowly drank the hemlock, he quieted them. He

had no fear of physical death, because he understood eternal life. Over 2,000 years later, his name lives on as one of our great philosophers.

Martin Luther King, Jr., in his "I Have a Dream" speech, knew he was going to be assassinated. He nevertheless had the courage to live for principles, the dissemination of which would cause his death

Mahatma Gandhi's fasting to end violence in India may have looked like inaction. He took no direct action to stop the violence. Instead, he applied a highly focused form of intention on himself. As Indian sects turned their attention away from their hatred of one another to an esteemed leader who was willing to die rather than participate in their dysfunction, the violence subsided.

Compare the power of focused intent that looks like inaction to the futility of oppressive, divisive, violent action. History is rife with examples of ineffective and destructive force: the Crusades, the Vietnam War, the Nazi regime in Germany, to name a few.

Every action-oriented conquering empire perceives itself as being right and superior, and its opposition as being wrong and inferior. It is divisive thinking that never succeeds in creating cooperation, peace, and harmony. It uses separation in an effort to control. It supports me/you solutions, rather than win/win solutions. Everybody loses, including the conqueror. Often, the conqueror is the biggest loser, because his conquest spawns opposition and lack of cooperation.

From an emotional perspective, what is it that drives this divisive thinking and conduct? Is it because we are all afraid—afraid of loss of approval, loss of personal power, and physical death? Is it because we don't yet see ourselves as part of eternal life?

From a non-dual consciousness perspective, we are all brothers and sisters with the same human weakness—separation. We are separated from ourselves, separated from each other, and separated from our ground of being. We are separated because we haven't mastered our fear and separated because we believe our word illusions. Our worship of words and our subconscious fears cause us to react against others and see ourselves as more intelligent, better informed, and more moral. We use words to separate ourselves from parts of self we don't want to see, projecting those unaccepted parts onto others, whom we then judge. "And why beholdest thou the mote that is in thy brother's eye, but perceivest not the beam that is in thy own eye?" (Luke 6:41)

Since we've now eaten of the tree of knowledge, our worship of words and our subconscious fears also separate us from the universal energy that unites us all. You can call this universal energy God, Higher Power, Higher Intelligence, nature, or even deny that it exists. It simply doesn't matter what word labels you use. The energy is there for anyone who chooses to turn the dial of his mind, body, and spirit and tune into it. It is the only thing that will eliminate fear. It is the only thing that will encourage win/win thinking. It is the only thing that will create powerful world peace, one person at a time. We all have only ourselves to work on.

A short rule for action is: take action only with yourself. Choose inaction toward others, unless they need your help and you are able to support their needs.

*Freedom*

Why do we dream of becoming free when
we have always been free.

We worship words and thoughts,
our own creations,
tricking us into thinking
we are not free.

How will we use our freedom?

# 17

# Science and Religion

*Hypothesis, Faith, and Creativity*

Language is only the instrument of science, and
words are but the signs of ideas.

—Samuel Johnson

More than one friend has warned me not to publish this
chapter. They want to protect me from the "steel and razor
minds" of the scientific community. If you are one of those steel
and razor minds, all I ask is that you listen impartially to what
I say, assimilate whatever you find of value, and enhance it with
your own finely tuned knowledge and perspective.

What I offer here is not an in-depth understanding of science.
What I offer is the ability to think and speak from a non-dual
consciousness perspective. This emanates solely from my mystical experience, thinking about it, and training myself in linguis-
tics. I have been studying the vagaries of language for thirty-five
years through journaling and writing. I also practiced law for
twenty-two years, where I had to think every single day about
how I was going to sculpt my words.

Because of my background and experience, I'll be writing
more about religion and spirituality than about science. That

is not because religion and spirituality are more important than science. It is simply because I understand them better. I'll leave most of the detailed thinking about science to the scientists, who are much better equipped than I to discuss scientific constructs.

Suffice it to say that religion and science are two different word/thought systems for structuring phenomena. They simply function in different experiential contexts. Science structures and gives meaning to what we perceive as physical reality. Religion structures and gives meaning to what could be described as human consciousness shifts.

The words science and religion have different meanings for different people. That, of course, is one of the themes of this book. That is why we humans communicate so poorly.

Let me clarify some of the different ways in which I understand the words religion and spirituality. I'll leave the definition of science to the scientists.

I think of the word religion as a formalized, doctrinaire body of thought. In its broader sense, it can also be used to refer to the symbolic art of a mystical experience or a broader collection of word symbols, generally labeled spirituality.

Religious doctrine is often viewed as an end in itself. In a broader sense, religion and spirituality can be viewed as a means to an end. The end is not the doctrine. The end is individual personal transformation.

Just as scientific words and mathematical symbols are given meaning within the context of the physical universe, religious words and symbols can also be given meaning within the context of our physical universe.

But aren't religious words and symbols revealed?

Of course! They are revealed in the same way the meaning of Jesus' words was revealed to me when I had my mystical experience. I experienced a sudden consciousness shift. I had an aha experience. I experienced a sudden change in my understanding of the meaning of Jesus' words. I was suddenly able to put those words into an experiential context and relate them to what was happening between me and the man at the door (see chapter 1). The pieces of the Human Truth Puzzle suddenly fell into place.

However, I knew nothing about what lay beyond the boundaries of that human puzzle.

When this transformational, consciousness-shifting experience occurs, nothing in the external physical world changes. What changes dramatically is a person's perception of that external world. How does one use words to describe a personal shift of perception from duality perception to non-duality perception? Words just do not work, but, despite this, the experience is so magnificent that many have tried. Some of the religious and spiritual words used to describe this new state of consciousness have been salvation, grace, samadhi, transformation, oneness, self-realization, and awareness.

Non-dualistic spiritual activity, as opposed to religious doctrine, simply springs forth creatively and spontaneously, with no nay-saying or rigid structuring from the linguistic centers of our brains. While it often uses human-created, analytic, linguistic tools to express its creativity, it is never controlled or limited by those tools.

Time is a concept where we think of our lives as moving along a straight-line continuum, beginning at physical birth and ending at physical death. Eternity is a concept symbolizing an experience of infinite creativity and total unity with the universe, a merging into the energy that some have called God. It is very much a present moment state of being, a zero/infinity point, a timeless, featureless space. It is nothing and everything, a void and unlimited potential, a return to the Garden of Eden, pure existentialism tempered by wisdom and a conscience.

In the non-dual, consciousness state of eternity, there is no beginning or end, because each of us is part of a total creative energy. The limited physical form we think of as self was created from energy, constantly changes, returns to energy, and nurtures new forms of energy forever and ever. Is this what is meant by reincarnation?

When this non-dual state of consciousness is experienced, the words time and eternity merge into the experience of the unified state of consciousness. From this unified state of consciousness, the linguistic systems of the brain can use analytic tools creatively to differentiate the two words, as they choose. Analysis and logic are some of these creative methodologies. Poetry, symbolism, allegory, and metaphor are others.

The circle or sphere may be used symbolically to represent this consciousness shift from conditioned dual consciousness to non-dual consciousness to creative use of dual consciousness.

With this spherical symbolism, consciousness can be perceived as shifting from a single, conditioned, mental perspective at a point within the sphere to the unified, non-dual center of consciousness. From there, it has the potential to move outward in infinite, totally unlimited creativity. The creative movement outward is capable of touching any of the linguistic or symbolic perspectives within the sphere, but is not limited to those perspectives.

NON-DUAL CONSCIOUSNESS

CONDITIONED DUAL CONSCIOUSNESS

CREATIVE DUAL CONSCIOUSNESS

A friend of mine, a former chemistry teacher, who has also experienced this non-dual state of consciousness, describes it as a gray, featureless space, without time, directionality, or movement. Everything is just there, completely accessible. It reminds her of the quantum vacuum she's read about in *The Field*, by Lynne McTaggart. Specifics appear in awareness only if a reference beam in the form of a question is focused on a particular portion of the energy.

It also reminds her of a piece of film containing the recorded wave patterns of a hologram. Only when a laser beam shines on the film does an image pop out in three-dimensional detail.

When my friend was in her gray, featureless space, she was smack in the center of the consciousness sphere. At this zero/infinity point, a point that could be labeled non-dual consciousness, everything is whole and completely accessible. It is a consciousness space of unlimited potential, but also a point where nothing is manifest in the physical world. Every point outside the center is a unique and slightly different physical, mental, and linguistic manifestation of that central, zero/infinity point.

Those who have not experienced non-dual consciousness are often stuck in their mental and emotional perspectives at a single point within the sphere. Their mental and emotional conditioning has taught them that their single point is the true, right, and only correct manifestation. Their manifestation is not wrong. Their vision is just limited. They see only the one point. They do not see the whole. They see, but do not see.

Is this the meaning of self-righteousness?

By contrast, a person who has experienced the center of the sphere is aware of all the points in the sphere and able to choose which point he or she will manifest in the physical world at any given moment in time. From the perspective of a person stuck at one of the points, this free spirit is a chaotic, loose cannon, whose manifestation cannot be predicted and therefore, controlled. How terrifying for the person stuck at one of the points! The result is often an attempt to protect the single dualistic point both from the free spirit and from other dualistic perspectives.

Jesus was crucified by humans stuck at a single point in the sphere. Socrates was directed to drink hemlock by humans who had never experienced non-dual consciousness. Gandhi and Martin Luther King, Jr. were assassinated by men stuck at a single point of their own consciousness and human conditioning.

Non-dual consciousness uses both analytic and artistic tools to create reductive forms, thought systems, and possibilities that simplify and explain our lives. While these reductive forms simplify, they also distort. By increasing focus and objectivity, they remove the webs of relationship, subjectivity, uniqueness, and complexity that our minds cannot understand.

Non-dual consciousness perceives everything that ever happened—every thought, every experience, every emotion—as a potential for every human at each moment in time. From all these possibilities, it chooses the thoughts, experiences, and emotions it wants at each and every moment.

If one knows why and how to choose love, why choose hate? If one knows why and how to choose peace, why choose war?

If everything in the physical world manifests through relationship, then the person who has experienced non-dual consciousness and wants to help others experience this mind-boggling consciousness shift, will simply assume a form in the physical world that catalyzes movement in that direction. Force is never applied to the other person. Mental intention is simply applied to oneself.

If you don't believe that, perhaps you are not yet making conscious choices in each and every moment of your life.

When we function from non-dual consciousness, the linguistic portions of our brains become confused. We want to say I know. Simultaneously, we want to say I know nothing. Perhaps it is better to ask questions: What can I create? What can we create?

Religious and spiritual thought use unexpected transformational or aha experiences and thinking about those experiences to create their truths. These truths are tested by others who similarly have had these transformational experiences. The experiences are communicated through poetry, analogy, parables, questions, and other symbolic and artistic forms.

Scientific thought uses eureka experiences and thinking about those experiences to create its truths. Scientific thought is tested and reported by using observation, measurement, hypothesis, and theory.

Both methodologies use a combination of experience and thought. Both methodologies include the unknown. Both are subject to human error.

If we are all subject to human error, doesn't that level the playing field? Science is not right and religion, wrong. Religion is not right and science, wrong. Both, if properly applied, are simply valid, creative vehicles for improving the human condition. If improperly applied, both are capable of terrible destruction and loss of human life.

Improperly applied religion spawned the Inquisition and the Crusades. Improperly applied science spawned the bombing of Hiroshima and every violent war that has ever been waged.

Why not apply both methodologies, each to improve the human condition, each in its proper sphere? Why not simply practice mutual respect and non-violence?

Science is primarily the study of our external world. Religion and spirituality are primarily studies of our internal world.

Science encompasses mathematics, biology, physics, and chemistry. Its methodologies inquire about and physically test perceivable aspects of the universe.

Spirituality encompasses art, psychology, mythology, symbolism, the ethics of human actions, and the joy and pain of human emotions. Its methodologies, at some point, require a leap of faith beyond methodology into pure, intuitive creativity.

Proper application of science can be viewed as a series of sophisticated tools to make our physical lives more comfortable.

Proper application of religion and spirituality can be viewed as a series of sophisticated tools to make our emotional lives more comfortable.

All these tools manifest through creative functions of the human mind.

Despite their very different focuses and perspectives, there are parallels between scientific thought and religious thought:

- The possibility for human error
- The creative use of the human mind
- The importance of noticing and being aware of aspects of our physical spacetime universe
- Use of analysis, reductive words, and symbols to express something that is far more complex
- Discovery
- Paradox
- Agreement among many for confirmation of 'truth'
- Limitations on what can be known
- A point beyond which the human mind cannot go

There are other parallels between scientific thought and religious thought. At least some scientists and some spiritual masters view everything as energy that is constantly changing in form. The first law of thermodynamics states that you cannot create or destroy energy. You can only transform it. A scientist might label this energy "molecules in motion." A religious leader might call it "God" or "Brahman."

In quantum physics, former Nobel Prize winner Werner Heisenberg formulated a principle called the uncertainty or indeterminacy principle. He challenged the classical Newtonian rules of cause and effect as applied to subatomic particles, showing that it is impossible to measure both the precise location of a particle and the precise momentum of a particle at a given instant. Because we cannot determine the cause with accuracy, we cannot determine a precise effect. We can only calculate the probable effect through matrix theory.

Doesn't this sound like the trials and tribulations of a human life? None of us knows, with any certainty, what challenges we will face or how we will move through them. None of us can predict when or how we will die. Isn't this uncertainty the terrifying dilemma a spiritual seeker faces before choosing a leap of faith?

My friend, the former chemistry teacher, adds the following thoughts:

In scientific thought, there is a whole matter/energy debate about whether light is a wave or a particle. It all depends on the context within which the observer is viewing it.

A coin has two sides. We can't see both at the same time, although we can certainly flip the coin from one side to the other, from moment to moment, seeing a different side in each different moment.

The same analogy applies to social issues. Once we perceive a person as nice or vicious, brilliant or stupid, good or evil, we have limited our ability to perceive the person's other qualities.

William James, C.G. Jung, and other psychologists have already done much work in scientifically mapping this transformational human religious experience. This is precisely where science can make its most valuable contribution in reconciling and integrating science and religion.

## Global Harmony

Life is a sphere
with each of us
somewhere
in the mass of that sphere
striving to reach the center.

We can watch each other
touch each other
love each other
learn from each other
but when we uncenter and
lose our direction
we get in our way
and the way of others

The path you must follow
is different from
the path I must follow.

Only the center
can give us direction.

## In His Image
### (*Bridges*)

The left brain plods along
with its rigidly accurate logic
except for its premise
that always begins with "if."

The right brain will,
perhaps must,
make that leap of faith
from which it absorbs the courage to risk
absurdity,

creativity.

# PART FOUR

## *Words and Emotion*

## A Single Tear

A single tear flowing
cleanses
releases
merges with other tears
streaming in sorrow
rushes in rivers
sweeping impurities
out to the calm
of the infinite sea.

# 18

# Hate and Love

## *The Passion behind Action*

Life is a magic vase filled to the brim; so made
that you cannot dip into it nor draw from it; but it
overflows into the hand that drops treasures into
it—drop in malice and it overflows hate; drop in
charity and it overflows love.          —JOHN RUSKIN

PLATE II (*inside front cover*) is another famous optical illusion,
an ambigram by John Langdon.

What do you see in the unchanging lines and colors of this
ambigram? Do you see hate? Or love?

What do you see in the unchanging lines and colors of the
world around you? How is your mind choosing to shape the
lines, colors, odors, textures, sounds, and tastes of your life?
What word labels do you give to these chopped up portions of
your environment? Do you see sorrow or joy? Conflict or peace?
Hate or love? What would you like to see?

*Rain*

Tears dampen my cheek
washing the pain from my soul—
Refreshing shower!

# 19

# Despair and Joy

## Shifting the Energy

> Where there is joy there is creation. Where there is
> no joy there is no creation: know the nature of joy.
>
> —UPANISHADS

THE EMOTIONAL ENERGY OF despair feels very different from the emotional energy of joy (see Plate III, *inside back cover*). Have you noticed, however, how one mutates into the other?

Over what we've labeled time, our emotional energy shifts like a kaleidoscope of beautiful colors. Where is the dividing line between despair and joy? How can we shift the emotional energy coursing through our bodies from despair to joy?

We feel despair when people we trust betray us, when we don't know which way to turn, when our creative energy is blocked because we're afraid. What is it we fear when we feel despair? Are we afraid that we're not good enough? That we've failed? Do we fear the future? Do we fear what other humans will think? What they will say? When we feel despair, life feels like a terrible prison, with no way out except death. Our energy is horribly contracted and turned inward. Our minds are thinking negative thoughts. Despair is a living hell.

Joy, on the other hand, bursts forth in free and spontaneous expression, expansion, and explosion of our creative force field. There are no prison bars, no blockages. We're joyful when we've accomplished something new, when we've helped a friend, when we're immersed in nature, when we're making love with our beloved, when our negative thoughts have shut themselves down and turned themselves off. Joy is a heaven on earth.

Is it possible that despair and joy are simply different forms of the same life energy?

Perhaps we can only appreciate joy when we've experienced despair. Perhaps we can only be truly compassionate when we ourselves have suffered the depths of hell. Perhaps there is a reason for despair. It brings us to our knees and humbles us. It helps us realize we can't do it alone.

## 20

# Fear and Courage

### *Crippling and Supporting Energies*

"Yea, though I walk through the valley of the shadow
of death, I will fear no evil, for thou art with me."

—PSALM 23:4

ON SEPTEMBER 11, 2001, there was no television or radio in
my law office. I was working with two exceptional paralegals.
Our work environment was efficient, harmonious, and productive. Then the phone rang. My beautiful staff members became
gripped with fear, then terror, as their sons, daughters, sisters,
and brothers began transmitting blow-by-blow accounts of the
much-too-graphic news broadcasts. The paralysis spread like a
plague. What moments before had been a space full of dynamic
harmony suddenly became so emotionally dysfunctional that it
approached emotional chaos.

There was no change in our immediate physical surround-
ings. There was nothing any of us could do to prevent the planes
from crashing into the World Trade Center. Yet the emotional
energy in that office changed in a nanosecond.

What if we had been working in a nineteenth-century office before the advent of telephone, television, and radio?

97

Wouldn't the energy in that office environment have been different from our twenty-first-century office with all its modern technologies?

What was the difference?

The only difference between the two environments was the influx of terrifying and gruesome words, pouring through microphones, into the minds and imaginations of my twenty-first century employees. The staff in my twenty-first-century office listened to those words and allowed their minds and bodies to absorb that frightful energy. The staff in my imaginary nineteenth-century office had no phones through which those gruesome words could pour. There was no word plague infecting my nineteenth-century office and no frightful emotional energy to absorb.

Is it possible that there are some things we don't need to know? Is it possible there are some energies we don't want to invite into our lives? Do you think the 9/11 hijackers would have plunged their planes into the World Trade Center if they hadn't believed they would immediately become media stars? Why did we all support their dysfunctional behavior by giving it our undivided attention?

The Amish inhabitants of Lancaster County, Pennsylvania, neither believe in nor use modern electronics. Perhaps there is a very spiritual and religious reason for this seemingly strange choice. They simply want to quarantine themselves from the infectious, emotional word energy that plagues our modern world via radio, television, and Internet.

I am not advocating burning telephones and TVs. I'm not advocating censorship. I am advocating the judicious use of news reporting by modern media so that we don't contaminate the flow of positive emotional energy into our lives. This positive emotional energy is our birthright. Why does the media destroy it by reporting the most sensational and vicious news available?

Even if the media chooses not to temper their words, there are many functional ways of dealing with terror energy like that of 9/11. Spiritual masters throughout the ages visualize themselves surrounded by beautiful white shields that insulate them from potentially lethal energies that can paralyze hearts and minds. They detach from those energies, instead of absorbing them. Alternatively, they deflect them back from whence they came, just as the black belt karate masters deflect harmful force back toward its originator.

Perhaps 9/11 was a wake-up call. Perhaps we have spent too many years isolated from our fears. We became complacent, smug, and arrogant. Perhaps the terror plague we experienced on 9/11 awakened us to the need to stop taking things for granted and start appreciating the things with which we've been blessed. We all need to recognize how very interdependent we are and how grateful we need to be for every living moment.

Fear is nothing but bodily reaction to a stimulus. Would you like to be able to transform your fear energy into courage energy? Here are some things you can do.

Taking action with yourself is a major step toward alleviating fear. Notice your body responses as you do the following mind exercises. Just step aside from your emotional involvement with the words and notice what your body is doing.

Take a look at your own fear. What color is it? What does it taste like? What sounds do you hear when you think about fear? Notice the sensations in your body when you think about your fear.

When you think of a time when you were afraid, what image pops into your head?

What sounds do you hear when you think about fear? Explosions? Screams? Sobbing? Silence?

Now, give your body permission to relax.

What color represented fear for you? Visualize that fear energy (color) flowing out and away from your body, leaving your body empty and relaxed. Flowing, flowing, out.

Now, think about courage.

Choose a color that represents courage to you. Visualize that brilliant courage energy pouring into your body, coursing through your arteries and veins, and filling you completely. Know that you can now do anything you want to do. Keep that courage energy flowing until your body is full and can hold no more.

As you visualize this energy flowing into your body, squeeze your thumb and middle finger together. This is called an anchor. The next time you need courage, squeeze your thumb and middle finger together and visualize your very own courage energy coursing through your arteries.

What are we doing here? Releasing fear? Or absorbing courage? Both are mind power in action.

Usually, it's easier and more fruitful to bring the positive into our lives than to release the negative. Sometimes, however, it is necessary to release the negative first, particularly when it's so overpowering that it's disabling.

Let me give you an example of why it's usually more fruitful to focus on bringing the positive into our lives.

Don't think about an elephant!

What's the first image that pops into your mind? An elephant, of course. If I were to tell you to think about an elephant, an elephant would also pop into your mind. The question is, do you want the elephant there or not? If not, focus your thoughts on whatever you do want in your mind.

Fear that immobilizes is always the result of your mind projecting its illusory "what ifs" into the future. Sit down, right where you are and consciously bring your mind back to the present. The present is always manageable. If you are in danger now, you won't have time to be afraid. You'll simply act.

If you believe in God or some kind of Higher Power or Universal Energy, sit down, bring your mind back to the present, and let go and let God. If you don't believe in God or some kind of Higher Power or Universal Energy, sit down, bring your mind back to the present time and space, and give yourself permission to relax.

Think about your childhood. Was it a pleasant time of your life or was it so filled with terror that you resist thinking about it. Perhaps you lived a childhood full of anger and fear. If you find yourself resisting going back to fearful moments of your childhood, trust that you will only go as deeply into these experiences as you are ready to go. Know also that until you are willing to go to the depths of your fear, you will never experience peace, courage, and self-mastery.

Was there something your mother said or did that frightened you? What was it? How did you feel? How did it change you?

What about your father? Was there anything he said or did that frightened you? Was it important that you be frightened?

What did you lose by being frightened? What did you gain?

I can remember a time when I was three years old. I wrenched my hand out of my mother's and ran across Roosevelt Boulevard in Philadelphia, Pennsylvania. Roosevelt Boulevard is a major, multi-lane highway, connecting northeast Philadelphia with the Schuylkill Expressway.

I don't know which of us was more frightened—my mother or me. My mother was afraid she'd lose her only daughter and three years of her caring, loving energy rearing me. I was afraid I'd lost my mother's love.

My mother rarely spanked me. This time she did. I never ran across Roosevelt Boulevard again. Sometimes fear has a valid purpose.

Think about your teachers, priests, nuns. Did they say or do things to frighten you? How did it affect you? Is it possible that they, too, were frightened? Afraid of losing their jobs, their control, the respect of others?

Fear is an emotion that sometimes grips each of us. It is an energy that moves from person to person when we allow it to enter our bodies and then pass our own fear words on to others. It is just like the plagues of the Dark Ages. Are these choices we want to make? Are we even aware that we have choices about fear and what to do with it? What can we do with this some-times-paralyzing energy?

The next time you notice fear in your body, stop, look, and listen. Once you know something about your fear, you don't need to react mindlessly, spreading it to others. Instead, you can transform it into courage. How do you do that?

First, take a step back and just notice the fear. What does it feel like? What is it doing to your body? Are your muscles tense? Are your hands shaking? Do you have butterflies in your stomach?

What message is the fear bringing you? Is it a message to pay attention and watch what you are doing? Is it an old phonograph message from your mother, father, priest, or teacher, grinding round and round—a message that you've never tested through your own experience? Perhaps it's time to find out whether what they told you is true.

Once you notice the fear and decipher its message you can make choices about what you want to do with it. Do you like these feelings? Do you want to hold on to them or do you want to release them?

What if you want to hold on to them? You like the feeling of the fear energy running through your veins. Moreover, you want to share it with others so that they, too, can be afraid.

You've heard that a serial killer is loose in your neighborhood. You bolt your doors, lock your windows, charge your cell phone, sleep with the phone under your pillow, and tell all your friends to protect themselves. Presto! You've succeeded.

Fear is always the mind's projection into the future. The dreaded serial killer is going to attack you tonight, tomorrow, next week, or next year. Your fear places you in a victim role. You are at the mercy of your thoughts and the actions of others. The serial killer is going to take action. You're going to be a corpse.

This is not to say that you shouldn't take steps to protect your physical body if you think you may be the object of another person's dysfunctional thinking. Do what you can and let the rest go.

Your own actions, as opposed to your mind's projection of what others may do, always occur in the present moment. They put control back into your own hands. The choice of action must be conscious. Conscious action dissipates fear.

Allow your fear to be your friend and trusted messenger. Love it as you would a child.

Ask yourself what kind of fear you are feeling. Is it energizing or paralyzing?

During a single forty-eight-hour period, a submarine's orders were to go where no boat had ever gone before. There were only two men on board with enough training and experience to drive it on its dangerous mission—the commander and his executive officer.

Were they afraid? You bet! Were they exhausted after forty-eight hours of constant maneuvering and tough decision-making. They were close to physical and emotional collapse. Their fear was energizing, a powerful motivating force. Had their fear been paralyzing, their boat might have rammed some underwater object or caught on fire. Sometimes fear is a good thing. Their fear made them very careful.

I never used to want to look at my fear. It was too terrifying.

My mother used to say, "Don't be afraid. Be a brave girl." I'd pretend my fear wasn't there. If I showed my fear and my mother found out, would I lose her love? As a six year old, I was very dependent on my mother, and yes, I was afraid. Maybe if I pretended I wasn't afraid, my mother wouldn't notice and would still love me.

As long as I continued to ignore my fear, it kept pressing against me, shouting, "Hey! Pay attention! Notice me!"

When I noticed my fear and allowed it to take me to the depths of my terror, my energy suddenly shifted. Someday, my body was going to die. That's what I was really afraid of. If my body was going to die, what was I willing to die for? What I was willing to die for was exactly what I had to live for. I began making conscious choices to live life full out. This is not a dress rehearsal.

Is it possible that our fear of being different strangles the strength, love, and creative power that lie within each one of us? Is it possible that your strength, love, and power lie in those very areas where you are unique?

Here are some things I've learned about fear and courage. If you find them helpful, please use them in your own life. If you don't, please just put them aside.

- Know that fear is only lack. When you lack knowledge, fear fills the void. When you lack understanding, fear steps in. When you lack power, you become a victim. When you lack love and compassion, you can help neither yourself nor others. Educate yourself, empower yourself, love yourself, be compassionate toward yourself, and live abundantly. As you do these things for yourself, you will also do them for others. The world needs what you have to offer.

- Release your fear. Parents are good at teaching fear. "Don't run across the street. You may get hit by a car." Fear is always the result of your mind focusing on something in the future that will probably never happen. Gently bring your mind back to the present moment. The present moment is always manageable. This is the "Power of Now" about which Eckhart Tolle writes.

- Be courageous. Courage is nothing more than a decision to pursue your purpose in life. You are a unique human being. Others are not always going to see things your way. Sometimes, you have to say no to their demands. Say no and bless them. Your uniqueness is the gift you have to offer the world. Don't allow another human to strangle it.

- Always stay in integrity with yourself. Personal integrity is the most valuable asset you own. It is the only thing worth dying for.

- Be a spiritual warrior. Be aware that there are energies that will support your creative spirit and energies that will drain it. Surround yourself with supportive energies. When you find yourself in the midst of destructive energies, protect yourself. Remove yourself from those people and that environment. Being a spiritual warrior is little more than staying centered on your own creative path.

- Envision yourself surrounded by a beautiful field of white light that shields you. Notice how calm you feel.
- Make a conscious effort to detach emotionally from cutting, sarcastic remarks. Don't use sarcasm on others.
- Don't be afraid to say no when you are asked to take inappropriate action. If you don't say no, you may be asking for a painful universal lesson.

Fear is the greatest barrier to freedom. When you overcome fear, you can overcome anything. When all of us overcome fear, we will be living in a harmonious, dynamic, creative world. Each of us has only one person to work on—ourselves.

Here's another optical illusion.

The lines on the drawing don't change. It is only the way your mind organizes those lines and the meaning your mind gives to those lines that changes.

What do you see in this optical illusion?

A woman in one of my workshops saw total chaos. She was so upset by these black and white lines on a piece of paper that she didn't even want to look at them. She threatened to walk out if I made her look at them. Of course, I wasn't going to make her look at anything.

After we chatted a few moments, she recognized that she needed structure in her life. She relaxed when I told her I need structure, too.

Other people see devils or angels. If you see devils, you may feel fear. If you see angels, you may feel courage. Which would you rather feel? Courage? Then look for the angels.

It is the same with our experiences. What's out there doesn't change. What changes is what parts of our experiences we focus on, how our minds organize those experiences, and the emotional tones with which we color those experiences. Have you ever noticed how all these factors are intermeshed, each interacting with and affecting the others?

If you're focusing on the beautiful sunset over the water, you'll feel peace. If you're focusing on the creaking, weathered dock, you may feel concern.

## The Other Side

Digging deep
in the depths of my psyche
aghast

my terror entombs

when suddenly
exploding into brilliant light and play
astounded

my terror chuckles

# 21

# Anger and Inner Peace

*Flipping the Switch*

> Any person capable of angering you becomes your
> master; he can anger you only when you permit
> yourself to be disturbed by him.　　—Epictetus

Do you realize how closely anger and pain are related?
Pain is hurt and disappointment directed inward. Anger is hurt
and disappointment directed outward. Both arise because of
betrayed expectations.

Thoughts that accompany pain are, "What did I do wrong?"
"What could I have done better?" "What's wrong with me?"

Thoughts that accompany anger are, "You're no good!"
"Shame on you!" "You better get your act together!"

The only reason either of these emotions arises is because our
minds have projected an expected result into the future: you'll
love me forever; you'll do it because you said you would; it's
going to be warm and sunny tomorrow, and we're going to the
beach; I shouldn't have to protect myself against members of
my own family.

Then, when you are betrayed, or when tomorrow is cold and
rainy, you feel hurt or angry. You want to make someone re-

sponsible. The only thing responsible is your own mind. It has set you up to let you down.

Can anger ever be useful? Absolutely. It is a powerful motivator toward change and personal growth. What other emotion could persuade you to set boundaries for people who treat you with disrespect? What other emotion could persuade you to associate only with people who support you and treat you kindly?

If you notice your thoughts directed outward in anger toward another person, you can choose to hold on to that focus or choose to shift it to a more productive focus. Anger is always a messenger telling you there is something in *your* life you need to change. If it keeps coming up for you over and over, you just haven't figured out the message or made the appropriate changes in your life.

Be aware of your body when you're having thoughts of anger or are stuck in beliefs/judgments about another person being less than perfect. Is your body tense and tight, are your fists clenched, do you have headaches? If you want to stay in this unhealthy state, all you need to do is hold onto the anger and judgment. If you want to release this unhealthy state, choose to let it go—not because you ought to, but because you'll feel better.

How do you do that?

Often, you need to take action. Perhaps you need to talk with the person with whom you're angry. Perhaps you need to set boundaries and limits with that person and stick to them. You may need to end the relationship if it is continuously toxic to your life and wellbeing. Ending a relationship without violence can sometimes express the greatest love you can give. It's called tough love.

You may simply need to refocus your energies by asking yourself: Is this an energy I want in my life right now? If not, where do I want my focus to be? On going to the store? On helping others? On getting something to eat? On resting? On pursuing my destiny? What do I need right now?

I don't know about you, but I can only have one thought in my mind at any moment, even though the single thoughts go rapidly flying by from moment to moment. Why not consciously choose a functional one?

When you care for yourself by releasing dysfunctional thoughts, your own health naturally overflows to benefit others.

Here are some interesting discoveries I've made about my own anger. If you find them helpful, please feel free to use them.

- Allow your anger energy to change. Give yourself permission to just be with your anger and watch it transform. Notice how it feels. Notice what it does to your body. Ask yourself what loss you are grieving. What are you afraid of? What expectations that your mind set up didn't happen? If you don't like being with your anger, ask yourself what actions will alleviate it.
- Use your anger to integrate, first yourself, then your relationships. When you notice anger in yourself, ask what message it is bringing. What do you need to change? Do you need to set limits? Walk away? Find new friends? Can you release your anger by redirecting your focus? Can you release it without harming others?
- If you need to express your anger, own it as your own and seek ways of conveying it that will not tear relationships apart. An easy way is simply to say, "I feel angry." Remember

that reactive anger is like a nail driven into a fence. You can remove the nail by saying "I'm sorry," but the hole in the relationship remains.

- Visualize the person with whom you are angry as a lost, hurting child. That's exactly what they are. They have no idea what they've done.
- Use your anger energy to propel you forward on your mission in life. Anger can be valuable fuel to help you blast through emotional roadblocks. Use it the way engineers use explosives. Position it to remove the block, not the road.
- Transform the energy of your anger into constructive action. Your anger is yours. It emanates from your personal perception of what is happening around you and the expectations your mind has set. If you feel anger, what choices can you make to change the situation? Can you stay away from the people and places where you feel anger? Can you take a long, brisk walk? Go to the gym and work out? Beat up a pillow? Can you share what you are feeling and why? Can you change your friends? Your job? Can you throw yourself fully into creating a win/win solution?

## Moment of Truth

Insane with rage,
Betrayed by two trusted friends,
My fantasy grabbed a pistol and shot them dead,
Trashing them from my life and this earth.

Reason returned.

Was it I feeling this anger?
Was it I wanting to murder?

Never again can I judge a murderer!
Never again can I condemn in others
The fury I felt that passionate moment
When I lost my sanity
And found my truth!

*Doormat*

Today

I noticed
my anger and pain
directed outward,
blaming.

Again

I'd laid myself down
like a doormat,
walked on,
trampled,
scuffed.

I didn't deserve that treatment.

But who put me there?

# PART FIVE

# Words and a Leap of Faith

Difficulties show men what they are. In case of any difficulty remember that God has pitted you against a rough antagonist that you may be a conqueror, and this cannot be without toil.　　—EPICTETUS

## 22

# How It Happened for Me

### *Choosing to Believe*

He that wrestles with us strengthens our nerves, and
sharpens our skill. Our antagonist is our helper.

—EDMUND BURKE

As a child, I attended Sunday school at the Unitarian Church
of Germantown in Philadelphia, Pennsylvania. My parents had
migrated to Unitarianism from Presbyterianism and Meth-
odism. Both had rebelled against being forced to accept religious doctrines as a prerequisite to belonging to a spiritual
community. Unitarianism is freethinking and intellectual. It
encourages questioning, skepticism, and a search for deeper
and more comprehensive answers

That training has been a valuable part of my education.
However, there are aspects of Unitarianism that have crippled
my spiritual development. Unitarianism is skeptical of everything. For example, no one in Sunday school ever talked about
mystical experiences. When I had a mystical experience, I had
no frame of reference within which to think about it. When
I experienced fear, even terror, there was no one to talk with,
because emotions were just not discussed. There is a very dif-

ferent energy in a Unitarian Church from the spiritual energy I have experienced, for example, in Unity and Science of Mind congregations. I like to refer to the Unitarian energy as intellectual energy and the Unity and Science of Mind energy as heart energy. The purpose of this background is simply to provide a reference point for where I was coming from, mentally and emotionally, when I participated in the following personal growth workshop.

Before the workshop, the facilitator asked us to make several commitments—to ourselves and to the other participants: don't chew gum; don't interrupt; be on time; do whatever we were told.

I didn't object to not chewing gum. I rarely chewed it anyway. I didn't mind not interrupting, and I wanted to be on time. However, I absolutely refused to commit to doing whatever I was told without clarification.

"From whom are we to take our direction?" I asked.

"From any of the facilitators in the room," the lead facilitator responded.

Immediately, my Unitarian skepticism kicked in. It wasn't an answer I could accept. I'd had bad experiences following the direction and advice of other human beings. Moreover, history taught me that humans had directed other humans to murder, commit suicide, and lay waste to valuable human resources.

The facilitator refused to continue unless I agreed. The room turned surly.

Sue had paid a babysitter to watch her four year old while she attended the workshop. My refusal to commit was wasting her time and squandering her money.

Sam had taken time off from work to attend. I was wasting his time and money by refusing to commit to do whatever I was told.

Sue screamed that I was a jerk who was making her lose money. Sam began shouting and pounding his fist on the table. The facilitators walked out, leaving me alone with the other furious participants.

I was doing exactly what I was being told—but not by the facilitators and not by the other participants.

I had gone to the workshop because I wanted to overcome fear. I was afraid of criticism, afraid of anger, afraid of what other people would think.

I was skeptical of the concept of God. I couldn't believe in an old man with a long beard, sitting on a cloud with a thunderbolt in his hand, waiting to strike me dead if I didn't do some vague, unclear thing he wanted me to do.

Before I entered the workshop, I knew that if I refused to do what the facilitators demanded, I would incur the wrath of the other participants. I was terrified.

I felt trapped between two impossible and painful choices. Was I going to give in to my fear of human wrath and capitulate to the demands of the facilitators or stand alone and refuse to submit?

If I chose to stand alone, I knew I couldn't do it by myself.

Faith is not knowledge. Faith is a choice.

If I were going to overcome fear, I needed help. I didn't trust other people. I'd been betrayed too often! To whom could I turn?

Tears were streaming down my cheeks. I didn't want to ask for help. I didn't want to believe in something I couldn't understand and couldn't see. I didn't want to humble myself, but I knew I couldn't stand alone against the wrath of the other participants without support. At the same time, I had to say no to the demands of the facilitators in order to stay in integrity with myself.

In desperation, sinking to my knees, I cried out: to something, somewhere, somehow; to something I couldn't see; to something I couldn't hear; to something I couldn't understand, "God help me."

Suddenly, I was calm and centered. My fear was gone.

As the other workshop participants screamed and shouted at me, I felt no anger, no hurt, no fear. I felt only centeredness and love.

What is this thing called faith? Isn't everything faith? Whether faith in other humans, faith in God, or faith in self, it's just a choice, isn't it?

If faith is a choice, do you choose to believe in things that work or things that don't? Do you choose to believe in thoughts that make sense or thoughts that are nonsense? Do you choose to believe in thoughts that imprison you or thoughts that empower you? Which choice will you make?

## Prayer

May mind become conscious.

Mind creates its own emotion and conduct,
constructive or unconstructive.

May mind become conscious.
May it choose its creation.

*Reconciliation*

Fog
silently
jolts my senses
demanding reconciliation
of surrealistic scenes.

The ocean is gone,
erased by a single stroke of fog.
Sand alone
stretches to gray horizon
where once waves played.

Where is the ocean?

A silhouette of man and dog appear
where sand meets sky,
and suddenly I know
the ocean is there,
beyond the horizon of my senses,
reconciled.

# PART SIX

# *Words as Holistic Catalysts*

## Monastery of the Soul

alone
in silence
we think unlimited thoughts
breathe unlimited possibilities
commune with self.

together
with others
we share limited thoughts
limited possibilities
codifying the fluidity we call self
into words,
rules,
form,
anything solid to cling to,

graven images
we idolize.

feeling fear
afraid to face our fear

in ignorance
not knowing our ignorance

forgetting creation
from which all springs.

# 23

# Creativity

## Using Words to Create

So God created man in his own image, in the image
of God created he him....          —GENESIS 1:27

DON'T BELIEVE A WORD I write. My words are no more than
creative vehicles.

Your words, too, are creative vehicles. The next time you
think or feel or talk or act, stop yourself and ask: "Are these the
words I want to say? Is this what I choose to create?"

There are many ways to use our minds. The way we use them
creates our reality. Our minds have the ability to choose the
part of the optical illusion we want to bring into our lives, the
side of the coin we want to see, the qualities we want in other
people. Our minds can focus their laser beams on whatever aspect of energy we want to experience.

Pay attention to your own experience. Notice what you are
thinking. When you think the thoughts that are in your mind
right now, what do you feel? When you think the thoughts
that are in your mind right now, how are your relationships
working?

Would you like to change your feelings? Then change the part of the optical illusion on which you are focusing.

When you think, "I am the world's biggest failure. I can't do anything right," how do you feel? Do you feel happy, positive, energetic, alert? Or do you feel lethargic, negative, disgusted? If you'd like to feel happy and energetic, try thinking, "I can do anything I want. What do I want to do now?" Then begin doing it.

Would you like to improve your relationships? Then change your thoughts about the people you associate with.

When you think, "My friend Susan is catty. She's always gossiping about me," how do you feel about Susan? Do you like her? Do you feel like hugging her? If you really want a warm relationship with Susan, try thinking about how she brought homemade soup to your house when you were sick or how she always listens when you need to work through a personal challenge. Try thinking, "I am so grateful that Susan is part of my life." How do you feel about Susan now?

Please note: you didn't change your words because Susan deserved it or because it was the right thing to do. You changed them so you would feel better about you.

Do you want to hold on to your anger and frustration?

I asked a friend that question one day, and she became angry. (Guess she did want to hold on to her anger and frustration.) Her perception was that I was judging her as being locked into some position she'd be better off letting go of.

The fact is I didn't care how she answered the question.

If she'd answered yes, I would have said, "Well, go to it! Throw your whole heart and soul into solving the problems you are perceiving. It is probably part of your destiny here on earth. Spend every waking hour developing this destiny. When you're asleep, dream about it. Build your life around it. Learn the tools for dealing with it. It's all that matters."

If she'd answered no, I would have said almost the same thing in a slightly different way. "Can you just let your anger go? What matters to you most in this life? What can you do to move yourself in the direction you want to go?"

When you focus on what you want and how you're going to get there, your mind isn't able to focus on what you don't want, don't like, and can't do.

Of course, it's risky daring to focus on what you want. You might fail and people might laugh at you. Do it anyway. If you don't do it, you'll definitely fail. If you do do it, you'll have an excellent chance of success, even if it doesn't materialize in quite the way you expect. Your self-esteem will soar with each new challenge you overcome.

It is challenging and exciting pursuing your own destiny. You can never know exactly how it will manifest. When you think you know and try to ram your own limited perceptions through, you will run into energy blockages. Consider surrendering them to a Higher Wisdom that manifests in its own time and own way and always unexpectedly and spontaneously.

Here are some ideas for nurturing your own creative spirit.

- *Bring your unique thoughts, emotions, perceptions, and experience to the altar of life.* Do this with wonder, not judgment. There is no one on this earth exactly like you, nor will there ever be again. Do you realize what a marvelous gift you've been given? Stop hoarding it. It has been given to you to give away to others. Share this unique gift that is you with the world.

- *Climb your own personal mountain.* Overcome your fear of heights. Overcome your fear of being different. You are different and are intended to be different. Your unique differences are the very gifts you've been given to offer to the world. Overcome any feelings of alienation you may have because other people don't think and feel the way you think and feel. Revel in the differences. Respect the differences. Understand the differences. Learn and grow from the differences. We are all on different paths to the same unifying consciousness. Share the benefits and abundance of all your wonderful gifts. It takes courage to stand alone with your own perceptions, thoughts, and feelings, but you are never truly alone if you choose to believe that the universe is supporting you through all your ebbs and flows. The universe supports the tide's ebbs and flows. Why shouldn't it support yours?

- *Polish all the facets of your diamond personality.* Every life contains a multitude of realities. Get to know all of your own and nurture those you want to expand. Do you love your gentleness, your devotion, your spontaneity? Gently polish them every day so they may shine more brightly. Have you noticed your fears, your obsessions, your pride, your treacheries? Forgive yourself and be compassionate toward yourself. Only then can you forgive others and be compassionate toward them.

- *Play your role in life to the hilt.* William Shakespeare wrote, "All the world's a stage, and all the men and women merely players: They have their exits and their entrances; and one man in his time plays many parts." Is there a real you or is everything simply fantasy and illusion? Does it really matter? You have a purpose for being on this earth. That purpose is to create. Take yourself and your perceived purpose seriously, yet allow another part of you to sit outside and laugh at your seriousness. Be the actor (the emotional self), the producer (the rational self), and the audience (the passive self) of your own drama.

- *Make your play your life's work.* What fascinates you? What do you love to do? What activities can you immerse yourself in and lose track of time? These are places where your creative spirit is already at work. Enhance these and find a way of supporting yourself financially with these activities.

- *Know yourself well.* Keep learning and expanding. Believe you know everything and know you know nothing. Act as if you know exactly what you're doing, even when you haven't the foggiest idea. Believe in your perceived purpose. Trust your inner nudges. Continually fine-tune the rational and linguistic tools your brain loves to play with. Keep your head and heart in the present moment and bring them back when you notice they've strayed. Trust the universe and pray for guidance from a Higher Power you don't know exists. Is this insanity? It's about as sane as any of us is going to get.

- *Focus on becoming more and more functional.* Detach from other people's dysfunctions. You can't force dysfunctional people to be functional. You do have the power to work on your own dysfunctions. One of those dysfunctions is trying to run other people's lives. Another dysfunction is lack of personal centeredness and integrity. A third dysfunction is getting sucked into other people's fights or dysfunctions. Your first job on earth is to work out your own karma, not somebody else's. Until you are fully functional and powerful yourself, you won't know how to influence others to become more functional. Stay serene and detached when others are upset and fighting. Visualize a white shield surrounding you and protecting you from all that negative energy. Trust that others have the intelligence to resolve their own issues and if they don't, they'll reap the consequences. Surrender into the silence and allow the energy to manifest as it will. Give help only when asked, but when asked, give it if you can.

◆ *Allow yourself to feel your anger.* Sometimes anger is a stepping-stone to action, increased self-esteem, courage, and determination. Allow yourself to notice it so you can move on. Your anger is bringing you a message that you need to hear and decipher. If you allow yourself to feel your anger as soon as it arises, it won't fester inside or explode in reaction. You'll avoid feelings of separation, self-alienation, and other-alienation. Simply say to yourself, "Thank you, anger, for sharing. What message are you bringing me? What do I need to do differently?" Anger and compassion are simply different forms of the same energy. If you are not capable of anger, you won't be capable of compassion.

◆ *Trust your personal perceptions.* Distrust other people's words (including mine). News broadcasts, what your neighbor heard about John, advertisements, and press releases are nothing more than distillations of one person's perceptions. Listen if you want, but listen skeptically. Don't get emotionally involved with them. Do you become angry when you hear news reports? Be wary. Did you personally see the story happen? If not, be careful. The words you hear are a façade for something much more complex. If your anger emanates from your personal perceptions, what action did you take to change the situation? If you didn't take action, why not? Fear? Then you've got something in yourself to work on. If you did take action, that's enough. Forgive yourself for less than perfect results and resolve to learn from the experience and do better the next time. Focus your energy on things you can change.

- *Help yourself first and others second.* Every airline begins its flight with a message about oxygen masks. "If oxygen becomes necessary, put your own mask on first, then help children or others traveling with you." The same applies in every area of life. Until you are functional yourself, you won't be able to help others. Your first (and perhaps only) job is to put the focus where it belongs: on you. Get clear about your own needs, wants, and perceptions. Communicate those needs, wants, and perceptions to others, if you choose, but don't expect them to take care of your challenges or see things the way you do.

- *Keep an open mind.* This is a very self-serving mindset. You aren't doing this to be kind to others or because it's right. You're doing it to free yourself from the prison of rigid ideologies so you can be fully creative and continue to learn and grow. When you dialog with others, your own consciousness will always expand.

- *Dance the dance of your own consciousness.* Free your body to use your life force in its own creative way. Who says you have to be consistent? Consistency is a marvelous servant, but a terrible master. Just be.

- *Weave the colors of your own life thread into the tapestry of human consciousness.* Have you ever watched a weaver create a beautiful cloth with multi-colored threads of different hues? You don't know what the whole will look like when the weaver is done, yet each thread is vital to the overall result. You, too, are vital to this world and what it can become. Weave your colors brightly and in harmony with the other threads.

- *Communicate clearly with the important people in your life.* Good communication requires two people: a clear speaker and an attentive listener. As a speaker, be specific. Give examples of what you mean. Instead of saying, "That guy in the store was busy," say "John, the produce clerk in Albertson's who was stocking the romaine shelf, was running from container to display." As an attentive listener, ask questions when the speaker isn't clear. "Which guy? Which store?" "What do you mean 'busy'?" If I'm talking about the "guy in the store" and you're thinking about the young man in the jewelry store selecting an engagement ring for his sweetheart, my statement won't make any sense to you, and we won't be communicating.

- *Surround yourself with creative friends.* You can be creative by yourself, but you'll be exponentially creative when you develop dynamic interactions with others. Pick people of good will and intent. Pick people who have learned from the school of experience. Pick people who know how to live from the core of their being. Pick open-minded people.

- *Learn and grow from your mistakes.* Everyone makes mistakes. We're all human. How could you have done anything other than what you did, given your consciousness at the time? The purpose of the old reality you created then was to teach you the same age-old, human lessons about better ways of doing things the next time. This is called working through your karma. We all do it. That's what life's about. Moreover, you didn't create that bad karma all by yourself. You did it in association with others. Do it differently the next time.

- *Form mastermind groups.* Meet regularly, either in person or by phone conference, with like-minded people who can support you along your life path. Provide information and contacts to one another. Praise one another. Thank one another.

- *Forgive yourself.* Forgive others. We're all in this together. Please forgive yourself for the mistakes you've made. What good are you when you continue to beat yourself up? Forgive those who have hurt you, but don't forget what happened. Forgiveness has nothing to do with forgetting the hurt. You need to remember so you can protect yourself the next time. If you don't remember, you didn't learn the lesson the experience was intended to bring. Remember to be nice to the person who hurt you. Do it for yourself so you can move along on your life path.

- *You'll never know Reality, so learn well the many perspectives about reality and how they dance with one another.* Study the many facets of your own personality. When you've lived from all the perspectives and facets, you'll know them well and be able to recognize them in both yourself and others. When you recognize them, you can do whatever is necessary to bring yourself and your relationships into balance and harmony. When you are compassionate with yourself, you can be compassionate toward others.

- *Liberate yourself.* Liberate others. None of us gets liberated until we all do. It is all very simple. You have only one primary responsibility: to liberate yourself. When you free yourself from the shackles of imprisoning word structures, you will be able to model freedom and abundance for all. Do you think freedom is a goal that you reach and never lose? No. Freedom is a continual process of moment-by-moment choices. You are free now. You will always have new challenges. You will always have new things to learn. Stay aware and open so you can remain free.

- *Build an inclusive community.* Counter cultures simply create another we/them separation. Build a culture or community with other conscious people that welcomes and respects all who want to join. Exclusion or separation occurs only because of the limited thinking of those who either choose to remain outside or bar others from entering—those who are alienated, for whatever reasons, from a full community that welcomes the participation of all.

◆ *Risk imperfect action.* You'll learn from your mistakes. Are you afraid you'll hurt others if you express your creative spirit? There's always tension between fear and creativity. Release your fear to the universe and create in the image of your Maker.

◆ *Learn to accept uncertainty.* There are no perfect answers. So, what can you do? You can live! You can clarify and integrate your own thinking, purify your own intent, accept your own human imperfections and weaknesses. Know that others will understand your words and actions thousands of different ways, have the courage to put your words and actions out there anyway, and learn and grow from the resulting human dissonance. Trust that there is somewhere, somehow, an energy or power that your mind can never analyze or understand that will support you, comfort you, and direct your steps through all our human uncertainty and turmoil.

◆ *Be awe-full and awesome.* Awe is a marvelous word for the Mystery of Life. If you live in awe of this miracle we call life, your life will be awesome.

◆ *Sculpt the malleable clay of your life into a beautiful piece of art.* Given your current experience and perceptions, what can you do with your life? How can you structure it? How can you think about it? What action/non-action is appropriate? What messages are your emotions giving you? What needs to be done? This approach will allow you to choose compassion when compassion is appropriate, passive resistance when passive resistance is appropriate, tough love when tough love is appropriate, and boundary-setting when boundary-setting is appropriate. What you act on is malleable, but you, too, are malleable. Just as the clay you act on has its own limitations and requirements, so, you, too, have limitations and requirements. Learn what they are and respect them. You never sculpt alone. The malleable clay which is you interacts with the malleable clay you are sculpting. The result of the interaction is both meaningful and integrating.

• *Immerse yourself in the immediate.* There is only one point from which you can act. That point is now. Time is an illusion or a convenient creation of our minds. The past is history. The future is mystery. You can create them in your mind, but the only time you can act is in the present moment.

• *Believe in yourself and believe in your God.* Belief is both wordless and capable of infinite words. It is certainty coupled with questioning. It is dynamic stillness. It is both separation and unity. It is love, compassion, commitment, and courage.

• *Cross-check your emotions and impulses with reason.* Cross-check your mind with your feelings. Mind is not the whole thing. Emotions are not the whole thing. Use both, but do a cross-check before flying. When everything is in harmony, the action is right.

• *K.I.S.S. Keep it stunningly simple.* You are like a ship sitting quietly on the surface of still water. That is your core being. That is the simplicity of it all. There are no waves, no turbulence, no storms—just peace and harmony. Creativity happens as you move away from the ship and begin exploring all the unlimited and uncharted depths beneath the ship. There you find the complexities of light and dark, life and death, joy and sadness. Others may have been there before you and left their word charts and maps. Use them as the guides they were meant to be, not as what is really true. Play with what you discover, shape it, and be shaped by it. When monsters arise from the depths, you can always return to the safety of your own still ship on the calm ocean.

- *Remember that it's all about you.* You, as observer, make all the difference. You can see others as jerks, teachers, fellow human beings, or aspects of yourself. If you see others as jerks, you'll react with anger, blame, self-righteousness, and attempts to control. You'll see yourself as superior and become an arrogant judge. If you see others as teachers, you'll listen with respect and ask yourself what you have to learn, even if the lesson is painful. If you see a fellow human as an aspect of yourself, you'll feel compassion and view yourself and the other person as equals, regardless of wealth, job, possessions, background, or education. What do you want to see and what do you want to become?

- *Keep your focus on yourself.* When you are driving and someone tries to cut you off, what are your choices? You can see him as a jerk and become angry and frustrated. But why give your power away to a jerk by directing your focus toward him? Shift the focus back to yourself and watch your anger and frustration disappear. Are you driving leisurely or have you made a commitment that requires you to be on time? Are you positioned so that you can hold your course and assert your rights? How far are you willing to go to avoid a collision? If it's really important to prevent him from cutting you off, put all your energy into that and watch him back down. If you're not in a hurry, let him in. It simply doesn't matter. If he can cut you off regardless of what you do, let it go this time and vow to position yourself better next time. You're doing whatever you need to do, you're releasing your anger and frustration, and that is enough.

- *Stop "shoulding" on yourself.* There are no shoulds or externally imposed commands. There are only needs—yours and mine. The more of them we can satisfy, the more harmoniously we will live together.

*Renewal*

Soft Avalon bay mud
oozes through toes
soothes anxieties

as a crab scuttles away
seeking safety in the same muck
from which I seek release

Clams sucking the silt
pop clean in hands
dirty fingernails happy

as the cool tide swirls inward
over toes
rooted
homed

# 24

# Affirmations

## Using Words for Support

Nurture your minds with great thoughts, to believe
in the heroic makes heroes.            —DISRAELI

READ THESE AFFIRMATIONS EVERY day. Add your own affirmations and watch the miracles flow into your life.

- I am beautiful and I attract beautiful things into my life.
- I believe in myself completely.
- I have an excellent mind that can solve any problem.
- My health is excellent because I take good care of my body, mind, and spirit.
- I am a powerful person.
- My positive, enthusiastic personality is infectious.
- I am a winner.
- All of my efforts are productive.
- I am a success in everything I do.
- I am full of positive energy and people respond to me in a positive way.
- I am confident, relaxed, and poised.

- All of my efforts bring rich rewards.
- I encourage play and relaxation and I, too, play and am relaxed.
- I love life.
- I attract abundance into my life.
- I interact with all people and draw out the best in them.
- I empower all with whom I have contact to be all they can be.
- I fulfill my destiny and am provided with everything I need to do so.
- Life is fun.
- Life is an adventure.
- I open my heart and my arms to all who want to join me in this adventure.
- Together we create marvelous new worlds of beauty and laughter.
- I support and teach those who want to grow with me and I learn from those who know things I do not.
- Together we are part of the living God, fulfilling universal principals of love, respect, creativity and justice.
- We are all part of the universal creative flow.
- I am so grateful.

# 25

# Visualization

## *Using Words to Focus*

Whatever you can do, or dream you can, begin it.
Boldness has genius, power and magic in it.

—Johann Wolfgang von Goethe

You have the power to choose the thoughts you want in your mind. You have the power to choose your emotions. What do you want to bring into your life?

Find a comfortable place to sit. Relax your body. Allow your hands to rest loosely on your knees, palms up. Allow the supportive energies of the universe to flow into your body. They are here to love you and caress you. Feel their warmth. Allow them to nurture and relax you.

Focus on the toes of your right foot. Relax the muscles of your toes. Just let them go and hang limp.

Now, focus on the rest of your right foot. Let it relax and breathe. Focus on the muscles of your right heel. Give your heel permission to relax and let go.

Focus on the muscles of your right calf. Release any tension you feel.

Focus on your right knee and thigh. Allow them to give up their tenseness. They can take it back the next time you go to the gym to exercise.

Focus on your right hip. Let it smile and breathe.

Now focus on your left foot. Allow your toes to let go.

Focus on the arch of your left foot. Relax your muscles.

Focus on your left heel. Release any tension you notice there.

Now focus on your left ankle, your left calf. Let them go. Just release your control. Notice how good you feel.

Focus on your left knee and left thigh. Is there tension there? Allow it to pass out of your muscles.

Focus on your left hip. Relax. Any pain or discomfort you may have felt when you first began this visualization is now leaving your body, allowing your body to return to its natural relaxed state.

Your entire body, from the waist down, is now totally relaxed. All your tension and anxiety have disappeared as you give yourself permission to relax. You trust this process and you trust yourself. You are a good person, much loved by your family and friends.

Focus on your waist and your chest. Release any tension you feel. Let it dissipate into nothingness, for it is truly nothingness.

Notice your shoulders. Allow them to let go. Let your fingers relax, your lower arms, your upper arms.

Focus on your neck. Allow it to connect with the rest of your body in a deep, relaxed dream state.

Notice your face. Is there tension there? Notice your forehead, your eyes, your cheeks. Give your muscles permission to relax. Let your scowls and wrinkles subside. You can place them on your face again, if you'd like, when you finish this exercise.

Notice your chin. Drop your jaw. Let it rest and unwind.

Focus on your scalp. Visualize gentle, loving fingers massaging the tension from your thinking muscles. Let go and relax.

Your body is now in a calm, totally relaxed state. You are filled with love and trust, for yourself, for others in the room and for the entire universe. There is no space in your body for anything except love. You feel only love. You are peaceful. You are.

Ahhhhhhhhhhhhhhhh!

Breathe!

A few years ago, I made a wish list of things I wanted. One was a beautiful home overlooking the ocean, surrounded by tropical plants, fruit, beautiful flowers, and birds. I visualized Hawaii, couldn't imagine how I could ever afford it, put the list aside, and forgot about it.

Three years later, my husband and I visited Roatan, Honduras. We both fell in love with the island. He bought a condominium, and I bought a home on a three-acre parcel of land overlooking the Caribbean.

A few weeks later, in the middle of the night, I suddenly awoke with goose pimples all over my body. My Roatan home was the manifestation of my visualization, but it cost only one-tenth of what it would have cost in Hawaii. My wish had come true.

## Keys

It was easy with knowledge
to use words carelessly.

To change "I was naked" to
"You sinned."
To change "I share responsibility" to
"You're guilty."

It is still easy without Knowledge
to use words carelessly.

To change "I'm afraid" to
"Stop that!"
To change "I'm angry" to
"Shame on you!"
To change "I believe" to
"You're wrong."
To change "I'm frustrated" to
"Damn you!"

It is still so easy
to use words carelessly

and lock oneself out
of the Garden of Eden.

# 26

# Positive Thinking

*Using Words to Bring Peace to Your Life*

A vivid thought brings the power to paint it; and in
proportion to the depth of its source is the force of
its projection.                                    —EMERSON

"WHY SHOULD I MAKE up positive thoughts," you ask, "if I
know they're not real?"

Why not?

This is not about what you should do. This is about choosing thoughts to support you rather than thoughts to drag you down.

What makes you think your negative thoughts are any more real than your positive ones? Nevertheless, you have no difficulty allowing yourself to get mired in mucky thoughts all the time. Why? What are you gaining?

What do you want to bring into your life? Harmonious relationships, financial security, serenity? Then start thinking about these things and putting your thoughts into words. Start taking little actions, one step at a time, to make those things happen. Give thanks for the harmonious relationships you already have, the money you already earn, the moments of peace you already have, and watch them expand.

Don't take my word for it. Try it and watch it work. Notice the miracles flowing into your life.

It's fun to set aside an hour or so just to dream. Get yourself a big piece of paper, a pair of scissors, and some glue. Poke through some old magazines. Cut out words and pictures you like. Build your own collage on the piece of paper and tack it up on your wall where you'll see it every day. That way, you'll have a constant reminder of what you want to bring into your life.

*Dawn*

A cardinal trills
its welcoming reveille
through stillness of mind.

*Abundance*

Drop
    by
       drop
         by
          drop
the
   dew
     drips
       onto
        alabaster
Drop          lily
   by        petal
    drop
      by
       drop
the
  flower
     fills    flow
      to over  i
         n
          g
releasing
    to
      the
        universe
         what
          it
           cannot
            h
             o
             l
              d

# 27

# Awareness

## *Just Noticing without Words*

The ultimate value of life depends upon awareness.,

—ARISTOTLE

AWARENESS IS JUST NOTICING without emotional attachment or judgment. Awareness is watching what is happening around you without reacting to it. Awareness is just experiencing, just feeling.

Awareness is also noticing what your body is doing in response to external stimuli. Is your body tense and tight? Are your fists clenched? Does your head ache? Or is your body relaxed and flowing. If your body is relaxed and flowing, you probably won't even notice. You will just be.

When everything within and without is in harmony, you won't need any word tools to get you there. It's only when you're out of balance that you need awareness and other tools to bring you back and keep you in focus. Awareness also helps you stay centered and pulls in energies that will support you when faced with crisis.

Noticing tensions in your body will help you release them effectively. If you aren't aware of them, you won't be able to do anything to make yourself feel better, because you won't even know you feel bad. You deserve to feel good.

Often, tension means you need to take action. Perhaps you need to talk with another person. Perhaps you need to set boundaries or limits. Perhaps you need to walk away from an abusive relationship or remove yourself from an environment that is toxic to your wellbeing. Maybe all you can do is beat the stuffing out of a pillow or run on a treadmill. Any of these will help, and you are the only one who can decide what will.

Awareness can also serve to bring supportive energy to your rescue. Just noticing the good things in life will make you feel better and nourish your tired spirit. Gratitude does wonders for a bad mood.

Sometimes, you just need to go with the tensions you're feeling until you get tired of them and the energy shifts on its own. No one can give you the answers except you and whatever Higher Power you believe in.

*Blessings*

Silver rain strings
its tiny pearl droplets
glimmering beads
upon shimmering wire

Magnificent artistry
offered to all
but nurturing only
seekers who notice.

*Whenever You Feel Hungry, Angry, Lonely,*
*Or Tired, Ask Yourself:*

What do I think?
What do I feel?
What do I need?
What are my choices?

When you answer those questions and meet those needs, you
will feel centered again and be able to help others.

# 28

# Choice

## *Using Words to Decide*

You cannot prevent the birds of sorrow from flying
over your head, but you can prevent them from
building nests in your hair.    —Chinese Proverb

Did you know you always have choices?

Regardless of what is going on around you, you are free if you
know you can choose.

Picture yourself in a dark, dank prison. A guard is holding a
gun to your head and threatening to pull the trigger if you don't
tell him where your friends are. Are you terrified? Do you feel
like a helpless victim? You are not a helpless victim if you stay
centered and make choices.

What choices do you have in this difficult situation?

You certainly have the choice of telling the guard where your
friends are, hoping he will spare your life, but how likely is this
desperate man to spare your life once he has the information he
wants? Even if he does, will you be able to live with yourself for
the rest of your days, knowing that you betrayed your friends
and perhaps contributed to their deaths? Can you trust a man
who is holding a gun to your head?

You can treat him with kindness and respect, even if he is holding a gun to your head—perhaps even because he is holding a gun to your head. You can try to engage him in conversation and develop some kind of personal rapport. Is there something you can do for him, short of betraying your friends and your own integrity? Does this sound like "Resist not evil, but turn the other cheek"? Yes, it does, and you can't imagine how effective it is until you've tried it.

You can remain silent and passively resistant, putting the burden on him for the next decision. Will he pull the trigger and destroy his only source of information? Probably not.

If you are physically strong, you may be able to trip him, punch him, grab his gun, scratch his eyes out, and physically release yourself. Only you can evaluate your likelihood of success if you make this choice.

Finally, you can silently pray for wisdom and courage.

Do you have any doubt that your body will some day die?

If you accept the fact that your body is going to die, what values are you willing to die for? The very values you're willing to die for are the same values you must live for, every moment of every day. If you make choices to live for those values, when your body does die, however that happens, you will be spiritually free.

In difficult situations, always stay in integrity with yourself. It's the most important thing you can ever do.

Do you realize how important it is for each and every one of us to make choices that create peace and harmony in our own lives? If every single one of us did this, only for ourselves, we would all be living in a peaceful, harmonious world.

Choice and responsibility lie within each and every one of us. You have the choice of thinking negative, divisive thoughts or positive, harmonious thoughts. You have the choice of using divisive words or supportive words. You have the choice of punching people with whom you're angry or walking away from them. Which is better for you? Which is better for the world?

Would you rather hold onto your anger and allow it to imprison you or release it in non-destructive ways? If you choose to hold on to it, enjoy yourself, but please, stay out of my life.

Our energies can work together or at cross-purposes. Your energy and my energy can create chaos, confusion, and discord or teamwork and harmony. If you choose to create chaos, please go out in the desert and do it by yourself. I will not permit you to bring chaos into my life. I hope no one else does either. If you choose to create harmony, please join the rest of us who would like to live in a peaceful, prosperous, dynamic world.

*Facets*

Within my being I hold the

terror of the coward
violence of the criminal
obsession of the addict, the

gentleness of the parent
devotion of the spouse
spontaneity of the child

I embrace the

ecstasy of the lover
neediness of the thief
ruthlessness of the dictator

treachery of Judas
intellect of Socrates
compassion of Christ

To which facets of self
do I choose to give form?

# 29

# Living in the Present Moment

## *The Time is Now*

> The secret of health for both mind and body is not
> to mourn for the past, not to worry about the future,
> or not to anticipate troubles, but to live the present
> moment wisely and earnestly.　　　　—BUDDHA

BEGIN WHERE YOU ARE and notice what is around you. What do you see? What do you hear? Smell? Taste? Feel?

Notice the thoughts flowing through your mind. Are they related to what is in and around you now? Or is your head someplace else?

Is your head in the past? Are you thinking about how arrogant Joe was yesterday? Or how your mom spanked you as a kid? Or how selfishly your ex-wife grabbed your money and the kids, too?

If your thoughts are in the past, you're giving your present power away.

Is your head in the future? What will my friends think of me if I do that? He's going to be angry when he finds out what I did. She better stop using drugs or she's going to kill herself.

If your thoughts are in the future, you're also giving your present power away. The only time you can take effective action is now.

Is your mental focus on what's going on in and around you now and what kind of effective action you can take now? Or are you focusing on what somebody else is doing, was doing, will do? When you focus on others, you give them your power. Don't give anybody free rent in your head. Allow them to earn their right to be there when they treat you with accountability and respect.

If you have the guts to pay attention to what you're feeling right now, what are you feeling? Anger? Fear? Anxiety? Resentment? Guilt? If you're feeling any of this stuff, what are you going to do with it? Does it feel good? Are you going to hold on to it and suffer? What is the payoff for holding on to it? Does it make people notice you? Does it make you feel right? Important?

Okay, immerse yourself in it! But be honest with yourself and notice what is happening inside and what you're getting out of it and what you're not.

Tired of pain and suffering yet? Want to find ways of releasing this stuff and letting it go? Once you get tired of it, it's pretty easy to throw it in the trashcan. But as long as you still love it, are getting a payoff from it, and want to keep it, you will.

If you're feeling joy, serenity, and love, your mind isn't going at all. You're just experiencing freedom and spontaneity.

Think about it. Is there any other moment except the moment your mind is creating right now?

How are you going to use your present moment before it ticks away?

Are you going to use your present moment to try to change others over whom you have no power? Or are you going to use your present moment to change yourself, the only person you truly can change?

*Today*

Today

I noticed myself
worrying
about future catastrophes,

Missing

the brilliant sun
shining on azure bays

Now.

# 30

# I Win, You Win, We All Win

## *The Best of All Worlds*

Enough shovels of earth . . . . . . . . . . . . a mountain.
Enough pails of water . . . . . . . . . . . . . . a river.

CHINESE PROVERB

FREE, DYNAMIC, POWERFUL INDIVIDUALS in a free, dynamic, powerful community walk a tightrope. Each and every tightrope walker must always consciously focus on balance. What if one begins to unbalance? The whole rope collapses with devastating consequences to all.

How do we hold the balance?

There is one simple rule: Do whatever you want as long as you aren't hurting anyone, including yourself. This is similar to the Buddhist admonition, "Do no harm." The rule provides an easy, if oversimplified focus. This rule is the line between anarchy and heaven on earth.

There are two simple words that create heaven on earth instead of anarchy: tolerance and non-violence. Both must be put into action.

There are two simple actions each of us must continually implement in our own lives:

1. We must allow our own unique, creative spirit to manifest; and
2. We must be willing to say no to other confused, divided, agonized humans, who are trying to control and constrict our lives.

Is world peace a real possibility? Absolutely, but it requires the participation of every human on this planet. It will manifest only when each of us is willing to take off our blinders, let go of our rigid thinking, and move toward the center of our own creative consciousness, using words and thoughts as creative tools, not entombing prisons.

In ropes courses, each member of a belay team helps steady the person walking the rope or jumping from the eagle pole. A woman walks the rope, twenty feet off the ground, steadied only by her own focus, the support of the other participants, and the ropes between her and the belay team below. A man slowly straightens himself up on the top of a high eagle pole, declares to the world what burden he is releasing or what mission he is accepting, and jumps—his fall broken only by his belay team below. Everyone stays conscious and in the moment. Everyone is focused on success. Everyone is working together.

This is true teamwork. In this sense, we really are our brother's keeper.

Each of us is offered the same opportunity:

- to become the fully creative person we were intended to be;
- to share our thoughts, emotions, and experiences;

- to accept the release of negative emotion from ourselves and others with detachment, forgiveness, and non-retaliation; and
- to use our creative ability to unify a divided earth.

If each of us made these choices only for ourselves, we would all be living in a peaceful, powerful, prosperous world.

## It Is All Very Simple

Each of us has only one soul to fix…
Each of us has only one heart to heal…
Each of us has only one head to clear…

our own.

But we need all of us.

Without one, there is disorder…
Without one, there is imperfection…
Without one, there is a hole in harmony…

no whole.

It is all very simple.
We all matter.

# Cities

> Therefore is the name of it called Babel; because
> the Lord did there confound the language of all the
> earth.                                    —GENESIS 11:9

> Thus with violence shall that great city Babylon be
> thrown down, and shall be found no more at all.
>                                    —REVELATION 18:21

> And he carried me away in the spirit to a great and
> high mountain, and shewed me that great city, the
> Holy Jerusalem, descending out of heaven from
> God....                              —REVELATION 21:10


Words,
bricks of the Tower of Babel,
glued together by human mortar,
struggle toward Heaven like Sisyphus,
only to tumble divided to the depths of Hell.

We have a City to build.

We search for bricks
but find only bricks of Babylon,
the polarized language of humankind.

Our City is complex, holistic,
a gestalt of inexpressible relationships.

How does one describe the color blue
or the smell of lilacs?
How does one share the warmth of a hug
or the pain of prejudice?

As we ponder the impossible in silence,
the City of Jerusalem descends,
each life a precious gem of shifting facets
kaleidoscoping through moments in time,
bound to each and one another
by the mortar of eternity.

We have a City to build.

# PART SEVEN

## Synthesis—A Final Word

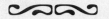

# Synthesis

Jesus—Christ—thesis
Nietzsche—Antichrist—antithesis
Hegel's dialectic—a tool for synthesis!

Übermensch[1]—the meaning of the earth!
What have we done to overcome?

To him that overcometh
will I give to eat
of the tree of life.[2]

To him that overcometh
will I give power
over the nations.[3]

To him that overcometh
will I give to eat
of the hidden manna.[4]

1   Friedrich Nietzsche, "Thus Spoke Zarathustra," in *The Portable Nietzsche*, trans. and ed. Walter Kauffmann (New York: The Viking Press, 1954).

2   *The Holy Bible*, King James Version (Cleveland and New York: The World Publishing Company), Rev. 2:7.

3   Id., Rev. 2:26.

4   Id., Rev. 2:17.

Übermensch—
The meaning of the earth!
What have we done to overcome?

How could anything
originate out of its opposite?
Perhaps
antitheses do not exist
or perhaps
they are merely provisional perspectives.[5]

Jesus came forth
and Pilate said,
"Ecce homo."[6]

Nietzsche came forth
writing
"Ecce Homo."[7]

But hearing,
they heard not.
Neither did they understand.

5  Friedrich Nietzsche, "Beyond Good and Evil," in *The Philosophy of Nietzsche*, trans. Helen Zimmern (New York: The Modern Library, Random House, Inc., 1954), 382.

6  *The Holy Bible*, King James Version (Cleveland and New York: The World Publishing Company), John 19:5. The Latin words *ecce homo* mean "here is the man."

7  Friedrich Nietzsche, "Ecce Homo," in *The Philosophy of Nietzsche*, trans. Clifton P. Fadiman, (New York, The Modern Library, Random House, Inc., 1954).

I am Alpha and Omega,
the beginning
and the end.[8]

Babylon the Great is fallen,
and she shall be utterly
burned with fire.

Woe unto this great city,
for in one hour
her judgment is come.[9]

I am Alpha and Omega,
the beginning
and the end.

Übermensch,
the meaning of the earth!
What have we done to overcome?

8  *The Holy Bible*, King James Version (Cleveland and New York: The World Publishing Company), Rev. 1:8, Rev. 21:6, Rev. 22:13.

9  Id., Rev. 14:8; Friedrich Nietzsche, "Thus Spoke Zarathustra," in *The Portable Nietzsche*, trans. and ed. Walter Kauffmann (New York: The Viking Press, 1954), 290.

# 31

# Antichrist and Christ

## *Hegel's Dialectic*

I know my destiny. Some day my name will be
bound up with the recollection of something
terrific—of a crisis quite unprecedented, of the most
profound clash of consciences....

... it seems to me indispensable to declare here who
and what I am. As a matter of fact, this should be
pretty well known already, for I have not allowed
myself to be "without witness." But the disparity
between the greatness of my task and the smallness
of my contemporaries is made plain by the fact that
people have neither heard me nor seen me....

... I am the Antichrist.

—FRIEDRICH WILHELM NIETZSCHE

GEORG WILHELM FRIEDRICH HEGEL was a famous early-nineteenth century philosopher. He developed a method of thought called the dialectical method, which posited that progress occurs through the conflict of opposites. First, there is an idea, called the thesis. Because the thesis is always incomplete, it draws forth an opposite idea, called the antithesis. Thesis and antithesis then become reconciled through a third, more encompassing idea, called synthesis.

Do you know what anamorphic art is?

Anamorphic art was used extensively in the seventeenth and eighteenth centuries to hide political messages that might subject their proponents to torture or death. The concept can be analogized to optical illusions in that the hidden meaning can only be seen from a certain perspective. It can also be analogized to the laser beam of the hologram, where an image manifests only when the laser beam shines on it.

Friedrich Nietzsche, a famous mid-to-late nineteenth century philosopher, wrote anamorphic philosophy, using Hegel's dialectic as a vehicle. Few have seen the hidden meaning in his words.[10]

Nietzsche was well aware of the illusory nature of words. His writings are laden with phrases such as, "They do not understand me: I am not the mouth for these ears."[11] "But why do I

10 One of the few who appears to have seen the hidden message in Nietzsche's writings is Hermann Hesse, author of *Siddhartha*, a novel that portrays a man's search for final answers. In another of his novels, *Demian*, Hesse wrote: "...on my table lay a few volumes of Nietzsche. I lived with him, sensed the loneliness of his soul, perceived the fate that had propelled him on inexorably; I suffered with him, and rejoiced that there had been one man who had followed his destiny so relentlessly. ... (W)hat nature wants of man stands indelibly written in the individual, in you, in me. It stood written in Jesus, it stood written in Nietzsche." Hermann Hesse, *Demian*, trans. Michael Roloff and Michael Lebeck, (Toronto: Bantam Books, 1981), 112, 116.

11 Friedrich Nietzsche, "Thus Spoke Zarathustra," in *The Portable Nietzsche*, trans. and ed. Walter Kauffmann (New York: The Viking Press, 1954), 130.

speak where nobody has *my* ears?"[12] He knew he couldn't use language directly to communicate his wisdom, but he could use it creatively to portray himself as antithesis, while, at the same time, sprinkling his writings with clues that would enable others to synthesize.

Nietzsche wrote: "Everything that is profound loves the mask.... Should not the *contrary* only be the right disguise for the shame of a God to go about in?... Every profound spirit needs a mask; nay, more, around every profound spirit there continually grows a mask, owing to the constantly false, that is to say *superficial* interpretation of every word he utters, every step he takes, every sign of life he manifests."[13]

Nietzsche waited, unmasked and unrecognized for over one hundred years. He knew that someday someone else would experience the same experience, think the same thoughts, and arrive intellectually at the same paradoxical conclusion. His writings would then become an instrument for synthesis.

Nietzsche wrote, "I know both sides, for I am both sides." [14]

Nietzsche gave himself the human label "Antichrist."[15] The label sounds like the antithesis of the label "Christ." Few have understood Nietzsche, Jesus Christ, linguistic thesis. Nietzsche

12 Id., 283.

13 Friedrich Nietzsche, "Beyond Good and Evil," in *The Philosopy of Nietzsche*, trans. Helen Zimmern (New York: The Modern Library, 1927), 425–426.

14 Friedrich Nietzsche, "Ecce Homo," in *The Philosophy of Nietzsche*, trans. Clifton P. Fadiman, (New York: Random House, Inc., The Modern Library, 1927), 817.

15 Id., 858.

Antichrist, linguistic antithesis. Two different word labels for the same, non-dual spiritual consciousness.

Nietzsche's words, "I am the Antichrist" come from his essay, "Ecce Homo."[16] "Ecce homo" were Pontius Pilate's words when he handed Jesus over to be crucified. (John 19:5). These Latin words mean "Here is the man."

Nietzsche wrote:

> "How could anything originate out of its opposite? ... This mode of reasoning discloses the typical prejudice by which metaphysicians of all times can be recognized.... The fundamental belief of metaphysicians is the belief in antitheses of values. It never occurred even to the wariest of them to doubt here on the very threshold (where doubt, however, was most necessary)... For it may be doubted, firstly, whether antitheses exist at all; and secondly, whether the popular valuations and antitheses of value upon which metaphysicians have set their seal, are not perhaps merely superficial estimates, merely provisional perspectives.... It might even be possible that *what* constitutes the value of those good and respected things, consists precisely in their being insidiously related, knotted, and crocheted to these evil and apparently opposed things—perhaps even in being essentially identical with them."[17]

16 Id., 811

17 Friedrich Nietzsche, "Beyond Good and Evil," in *The Philosophy of Nietzsche*, trans. Helen Zimmern, (New York: Random House, Inc., The Modern Library, 1927) 382-83.

Nietzsche had struggled with the same mental, linguistic and emotional challenges with which I struggled after the mystical experience, the same challenges presented to Zen novitiates in the form of koans. Knowledge was crocheted to ignorance; truth was crocheted to falsehood. Was Christ crocheted to Antichrist?

Shortly after my mystical experience, I tried to express these crocheted concepts graphically. It came out like this:

GOOD / EVIL

ANTICHRIST / CHRIST

FALSEHOOD / TRUTH / GOD

LOVE / HATE

PEACE / CONFLICT

SKEPTICISM / FAITH

BEGINNING / END

How does one separate these insidiously knotted concepts? No matter what form one chooses to express non-dual spiritual consciousness, the form is only a single creative part of the whole, a single linguistic and symbolic expression of that which contains the possibility of an infinite number of linguistic and symbolic expressions.

Did Nietzsche put on the outer garments and trappings of the Antichrist to symbolize the linguistic divisiveness of the human experience? It was surely a disguise that no one who thought divisively could penetrate. It was a disguise that only individuals who had experienced the unity underlying linguistic form could access.

While Nietzsche's words took the form of antithesis, they were sprinkled with clues pointing to the identical and creative nature of truth and falsehood, knowledge and ignorance, Christ and Antichrist.

One of Nietzsche's themes was "the overman."[18] "Behold, I teach you the overman. The overman is the meaning of the earth. Let your will say: the overman shall be the meaning of the earth."[19]

How strikingly these words parallel the words in the Christian Bible's Book of Revelation.

"To him that overcometh will I give to eat of the tree of life." (Rev. 2:7) "He that overcometh shall not be hurt of the second

18 The German word for overman is Übermensch. In some translations of "Thus Spake Zarathustra," Übermensch has been improperly translated Superman.

19 Friedrich Nietzsche, "Thus Spoke Zarathustra," in *The Portable Nietzsche*, trans. and ed. Walter Kaufmann (New York: The Viking Press, 1954), 125.

death." (Rev. 2:11) "To him that overcometh will I give to eat of the hidden manna, and will give him a white stone, and in the stone a new name written, which no man knoweth saving he that receiveth it." (Rev. 2:17) "And he that overcometh and keepeth my works unto the end, to him will I give power over the nations." (Rev. 2:26) "He that overcometh, the same shall be clothed in white raiment." (Rev. 3:5) "Him that overcometh will I make a pillar in the temple of my God, and he shall go no more out: and I will write upon him the name of my God, and the name of the city of my God, *which* is new Jerusalem, which cometh down out of heaven from my God: and I *will write upon him* my new name." (Rev. 3:12) "To him that overcometh will I grant to sit with me in my throne, even as I also overcame and am set down with my Father in his throne." (Rev. 3:21)

Did Nietzsche have Christ consciousness? Buddhist awareness? Was antithesis the only way he could humanly express the paradoxes within this human state of consciousness? Has he been unheard, misunderstood, and unrecognized, because the word sculptures with which he expressed himself were so unlike the forms that believers expected? Do we all have this same potential for Christ consciousness? Can we all overcome our conditioned thinking and change it to creative thinking?

Is it possible that the second coming in the Bible's Book of Revelation, the overcoming, has always been possible throughout that continuum we call time? The second coming and return to the Garden of Eden is an individual human consciousness shift. It symbolizes the ability of each of us to remove our blinders and attune ourselves to that creative energy or power that directs our lives harmoniously if we allow it to do so.

Friedrich Nietzsche labeled himself Antichrist. He peppered his writings with Biblical references and clues symbolizing his

Christ identity. Do his writings evidence the blinders our reductive, dualistic thinking straps onto our creative consciousness?

Do we see, but not see, hear, but not hear? Do we expect events to take a different form? Do we expect external things to change, rather than the consciousness within each one of us? What if we expect trumpets and brilliant lights and angels? Are we all wearing blinders and missing what is there for all to see? Is everything written in the Bible and other religious and philosophical writings simply artistic and symbolic expression of this expanded creative state of consciousness, available to every single person on this planet?

Is it possible that, when perceived through this expanded, creative, non-dual state of consciousness, that the events in the Book of Revelation occur, not 2,000 years after the physical birth and death of Jesus, but in eternity, where eternity symbolizes an altered state of consciousness, possible for every human at every moment in what scientific thinking perceives as time? This overcoming has always been possible, but it requires the participation of every human on this planet. When are you going to make the commitment to overcome and participate in the creation of a peaceful, powerful, prosperous planet?

# Epilogue

Friends with whom I've shared these thoughts have asked fascinating questions.

How do I feel about releasing my ideas after struggling, working, living, and playing with them for so many years? Do I feel possessive? Do I want to hold on to them?

No. I am ready to let them go.

They aren't mine. They have simply flowed through me like Akashic records. They are equally a part of anyone who is living through the same struggles and finds them useful.

Am I saying a universal system of thought is possible?

1. No, not a universal system of thought. Perhaps a universal consciousness or awareness, a universal resonance or attraction.

Alternatively...

2, Yes, but only if that universal system of thought recognizes mind, language, and perception as variables of the system.

Can the question be rephrased in a more meaningful way? Is there a universal perspective that encompasses all systems of thought?

The answer to that question is a resounding "Yes!"

What is that universal perspective?

It is a perspective that is beyond words and symbols. Words and symbols can reflect it. They can never fully describe it. Perhaps they can only catalyze it as adequately as is humanly possible.

# Bibliography

Al-Anon Family Group. *One Day at a Time.* New York: Al-Anon Family Group Headquarters, 1987.

Al-Anon Family Group. *Al-Anon's Twelve Steps & Twelve Traditions.* New York: Al-Anon Family Group Headquarters, Inc., 1987.

Armentrout, Douglas. *Canvas in the Mirror.* Boise, Idaho: The Creative Lure, 1996.

Bartholomew. *From the Heart of a Gentle Brother.* Channeled by Mary-Margaret Moore. Taos, New Mexico: High Mesa Press, 1987.

Beattie, Melody. *Codependent No More.* New York: Harper/Hazelden, 1987.

Bohm, David. *Wholeness and the Implicate Order.* London and New York: Routledge, 2005.

Chôdron, Pema. *When Things Fall Apart: Heart Advice for Difficult Times.* Boston: Shambhala Publications, Inc., 1997.

Davies, Paul. *God and the New Physics.* New York: Simon & Schuster, Inc., 1984.

Eliot, T.S. *T.S. Eliot Selected Poems.* New York: Harcourt, Brace & World, Inc., 1964.

Emerson, Ralph Waldo. *Essays.* New York: Merrill and Baker (no date).

Gibran, Kahlil. *A Tear and a Smile.* Translated from the Arabic by H.M. Nahmad. New York: Alfred A. Knopf, 1986.

———. *Jesus, the Son of Man, His Words and His Deeds as Told and Recorded by Those Who Knew Him.* New York: Alfred A. Knopf, 1973.

———. *The Prophet.* New York: Alfred A. Knopf, 1986.

———. *The Wanderer, His Parables and Sayings.* New York: Alfred A. Knopf, 1966.

*Great Dialogs of Plato. The Republic. Apology.* Crito. Phaedo. Ion. Meno. Symposium. Translated by W.H.S. Rouse. Edited by Eric H. Warmington and Philip G. Rouse. New York and Toronto: The New American Library, 1956.

Hermann Hesse. *Demian*. Translated by Michael Roloff and Michael Lebeck. Toronto: Bantam Books, 1981.

———. *Siddhartha*. New York: New Directions Publishing Corporation, 1951.

Holy Bible, The, containing the Old and New Testaments, Authorized King James Version. Cleveland and New York: The World Publishing Company.

James, William. *The Varieties of Religious Experience, A Study in Human Nature*. Modern Library Edition. New York: Random House, Inc., 1994.

Laszlo, Ervin. *Science and the Akashic Field, An Integral Theory of Everything*. Rochester, Vermont: Inner Traditions, 2004.

Leonard, George, and Michael Murphy. *The Life We Are Given, a Long Term Program for Realizing the Potential of Body, Mind, Heart and Soul*. New York: G.P. Putnam's Sons, 1995.

Lerner, Rokelle. *Daily Affirmations*. Pompano Beach, Florida: Health Communications, Inc., 1985.

McTaggart, Lynne. *The Field, The Quest for the Secret Force of the Universe*. Great Britain: HarperCollins Publishers, 2001.

Neill, A.S. *Freedom, Not License*. New York City: Hart Publishing Company, 1966.

———. *Summerhill, a Radical Approach to Child Rearing*. New York City: Hart Publishing Company, 1964.

Nietzsche, Friedrich Wilhelm. *The Philosophy of Nietzsche*. "Thus Spake Zarathustra," translated by Thomas Common. "Beyond Good and Evil," translated by Helen Zimmern. "The Geneology of Morals," translated by Horace B. Samuel, M.A. "Ecce Homo," translated by Clifton P. Fadiman. "The Birth of Tragedy from the Spirit of Music," translated by Clifton P. Fadiman. New York: The Modern Library, 1954.

———. *The Portable Nietzsche*. "Twilight of the Idols," "The Antichrist," "Nietzsche contra Wagner," "Thus Spoke Zarathustra." Translated and edited by Walter Kaufmann. New York: The Viking Press, Inc., 1954.

Prather, Hugh. *Notes to Myself*. Moab, Utah: Real People Press, 1970.

———. *There is a Place Where You are Not Alone*. New York: Doubleday, 1980.

Rico, Gabriele Lusser. *Writing the Natural Way*. Los Angeles: J.P. Tarcher, Inc., 1983.

Roberts, Jane. *The Nature of Personal Reality*. New York: Bantam Books, 1978.

Ruiz, Don Miguel. *The Four Agreements*. San Rafael, California: Amber-Allen Publishing, Inc., 1997.

Ruiz, Don Miguel with Janet Mills. *Prayers: A Communion with Our Creator*. San Rafael, California: Amber-Allen Publishing, Inc., 2001.

Schaef, Anne Wilson. *Co-Dependence, Misunderstood—Mistreated*. San Francisco: Harper & Row, 1986.

———. *Women's Reality, an Emerging Female System in a White Male Society.* San Francisco: Harper & Row, 1985.

Shakespeare, William. *The Complete Works of Shakespeare.* Edited with a Glossary by W.J. Craig, M.A., London: Oxford University Press, 1928.

Tan, Pilar, M.D. *Learning and Being: Thoughts on Overcoming Problems and Living Fully.* Roselle Park, New Jersey: Bright Light Publishing, 2003.

Tolle, Eckhart. *The Power of Now, a Guide to Spiritual Enlightenment.* Novato, California: New World Library, 1999.

Wilber, Ken. *A Theory of Everything. An Integral Vision for Business, Politics, Science, and Spirituality.* Boston: Shambhala Publications, Inc., 2000.

Williamson, Marianne. *Illuminated Prayers.* New York: Simon & Schuster, 1997.

Zukav, Gary. *The Seat of the Soul.* New York: Simon & Schuster, 1989.

# Index

Numbers in *italics* denote figures, poetry, and other short inserts.

Christ/Antichrist, *168*, 172–78. *See also* Jesus
Christianity
　Human Truth Puzzle and, 41–42, 81
　Nietzsche's Antichrist, *168–70*, 172–78
　*See also* Bible; Jesus
Church of Religious Science, 118
circle/sphere, *xviii*, 63, 82, *83*, 89
community, 3, 51, 117, 133–34
conditioned dual consciousness, 82–83
consciousness. *See* conditioned dual consciousness; creative dual consciousness; non-dual consciousness; transformed consciousness
courage, 99–107, *108*
creative dual consciousness, 62–63, *83*
creativity
　co-creation, *67*
　death and rebirth, *64*
　Human Truth Puzzle and, 41–42
　logic and, *90*
　nurturing creative spirit, 127–37
　tolerance and, 162–63
　using words to create, 125–26

death, *64*, 65–66, 154
despair, 95
devil, 55
dialectical method, *168–70*, 171–78
doctrine, 24, 80–81, 117. *See also* belief
dualism, 81–85, *83*. *See also* opposition

Emerson, Ralph Waldo, 60
emotion
　choice and, 155
　creativity and, 135
　as life energy, 95–96

mastery of emotional energy, 97–107, *108*, *152*
　sorrow as cleansing, 92, *94*
　*See also* particular emotions
end/beginning, *63*, 81–82, *170*
energy, 65–66, 75
Escher, M.C., *106*
eternity, 57–58, 63–65, 81–82
evil/good. *See* good/evil
experience
　language and, 15, 23–28, *29–31*, 39–40
　mystical experience, 5–6

faith, 59–62, 119–20
Fall, the (Garden of Eden story), 11–13, 28, *29–31*, 82, *144*, 177
falsehood/truth, 42–43, *45*, 85–88. *See also* Human Truth Puzzle
fear
　creativity and, 42, 95, 128
　of death, 75–76
　purposeful fear, 102–7
　self-awareness and, 57, *67*, 77, *108*
　visualization and, 99–102
*Field, The* (McTaggart), 83
focus
　anger and, 110–11
　awareness and, 149, 158
　balance and, 161–62
　creativity and, 126–36
　in describing experiences, 23–24
　fear and, 105
　mastery of, 27, *48*, 50, 72, 100–101, 107
　meaning and, 19
　non-dual consciousness and, 85
　power of focused intent, 76
　visualization and, 141–43
forgiveness, *67*, 130–33
freedom
　free will and predestination, *68*, 69–70

# *What Reviewers Are Saying...*

Atypical ideas, a new way of thinking, and the possibility of getting along better with others—that's what you'll find in Janet Smith Warfield's SHIFT *Change Your Words, Change Your World.*

. . . well thought out and intriguing. . . . SHIFT allows the reader to be in control and decide his own destiny.

—CHERYL MALANDRINOS, reviewer, *The Muse Reviews*

. . . a creative tool for expanding consciousness . . . not through rigid control, but through self-knowledge, awareness, and understanding.

SHIFT is not for the faint of heart. If you're looking for pat answers and authoritarian security, you won't find them here. If you're a curious, risk-taking problem-solver who wants to enhance your life and create harmony on our planet, it might just be the thing.

—*Monthly Aspectarian*

. . . an earthshaking experience so powerful and unifying that the author was unable to communicate it at the time, this book aims to catalyze the same experience in others by using words to bring peace to the turmoils of daily life.

—*Swarthmore College Alumni Magazine*

. . . SHIFT draws out new ways of thinking about old challenges. Its purpose is to bring powerful peace to the reader and, as a result, powerful peace to the planet, one reader at a time.

—Rutgers University, *Off the Shelf*